Guitarist's Guide to Maintenance & Repair

A Tech to the Stars Tells How to Maintain Your Axe Like a Pro

By Doug Redler and Dave Rubin

Preface by Dave Rubin
Forewords by Rich Robinson and Jeff Thall

Photographs by Kole Smith

ISBN 978-1-4584-1215-7

HAL•LEONARD®

Visit Hal Leonard Online at
www.halleonard.com

Contact us:
Hal Leonard
7777 West Bluemound Road
Milwaukee, WI 53213
Email: info@halleonard.com

In Europe, contact:
Hal Leonard Europe Limited
42 Wigmore Street
Marylebone, London, W1U 2RN
Email: info@halleonardeurope.com

In Australia, contact:
Hal Leonard Australia Pty. Ltd.
4 Lentara Court
Cheltenham, Victoria, 3192 Australia
Email: info@halleonard.com.au

Guitarist's Guide to Maintenance & Repair

TABLE OF CONTENTS

DEDICATION

I would like to thank all of the many friends, musicians, and technicians that I have met on my travels. Special thanks to:

Mom, Dad, and sister Leslie for all of their support and understanding throughout the years. Jodi Redler, Jeff Thall, Rich Robinson, Kim Hilton, Bill Thomson, Matt Brewster, Matt Wells, Eric Bradley, kd Lang, Dan Vickrey, Keith Strickland, Dave Russell (RIP), Matthew Murphy, Steve Jensen, Martin Kirkup, Hugh Gilmartin, Steve Christmas Chris Thomas Makoto Fukano (Freedom Custom Guitar Research), Bryan Galloup, Russ Olmsted, Sam Guidry, Jason Portier, Judd Goldrich. I would also like to thank Rich Robinson for the use of his guitar collection for many of the pictures in this book. And last but not least, my friend, mentor, and confidant Dave Rubin.

Doug Redler

PREFACE

He's not the star of the show, though the show would not go on without him. He's not a guitar hero, though he is an excellent player. No, he is the guitar tech who makes sure the wheels do not fall off the rock 'n' roll train. And if they should happen to become detached, he knows how to put them back on quickly and efficiently. He's not just any guitar tech, but the guitar tech to the stars, including Rich Robinson (the Black Crowes), kd Lang, the Dixie Chicks, the B-52s, Jeff Thall (with Bryan Ferry), Steve Stevens, Echo & the Bunneymen, Paul Simon, Goo Goo Dolls, Counting Crows, and Peter Gabriel, Heart, among many others.

Doug Redler is the man who has seen it all and knows exactly what to do when it comes to keeping guitars and amps healthy. Now he gladly shares the knowledge of his art and craft and reveals his trade secrets so that anyone with even passing mechanical ability can maintain their own gear. Short of major repairs comparable to fixing the transmission on your car, this book covers all the necessary aspects, from intonation to changing amp tubes and beyond, as comparable to doing your own car "tune-up" and saving the cost of a garage. The only caveat is that you may need two copies: one to have in your guitar case at all times, and one to give to your favorite musician or roadie as a Christmas present.

Dave Rubin
NYC, 2012

FOREWORD

DOUG "THE PROFESSOR" REDLER
By Rich Robinson

Doug Redler, the "Professor," "Red," the "Coach," "Hoss," and "Hot Sauce" are just a few of the names placed upon this man's sturdy shoulders. When Doug is not pursuing his first passions—watching hockey and eating pizza—he's devoted the majority of his life to the playing and care of guitars. I've worked with Doug for over 10 years now, and I have to say that he is great at what he does—with guitars I mean. (The other passions I'm not so sure about.)

Guitar techs really carry a tremendous responsibility. Frankly, without Doug working on my guitars, the show would not go smoothly. Loading in, setting up my amps and pedal board, changing strings, tuning electrics and acoustics constantly, putting out set lists with guitar changes, dealing with ever-changing set lists, making sure there are back up guitars, handling 15 plus tunings, keeping the amps and effects running, and dealing with vendors are just some of the things Doug does within a day. During the show, he's constantly tuning, watching, and listening for any problems that might arise. Amps go down, strings break, there are tuning and monitor issues, etc., and Doug has to be ready for anything. I'm very happy and grateful to have Doug on tour with me because I truly feel that he is one of the best techs around. I know that everything that needs to be done will be done.

This book has the interesting perspective of someone who has chosen this nomadic life in a traveling music show. Doug's love for music and for the craft of guitars is what fuels him. Read up, learn something, and enjoy.

DOUG REDLER
By Jeff Thall

In June of 1988, at the age of 23, Doug and I set out on a world tour with Bryan Ferry. It was the first tour either of us had ever done. At the time, I was playing in bands around New York, and Doug was working at *Billboard Magazine*. When I got the gig with Bryan, I called Doug and asked him to come on the road with us. I think he thought about it for about five seconds before accepting. So much for a career in journalism!

Rewind… our friendship started in the ninth grade when I came up to Doug in the school hallway and asked him if he wanted to see the Queen concert at Madison Square Garden. What a great first hang! It was the 1978 News of the World Tour. We were 14 years old and became fast friends after that. Listening to music, going to concerts, and playing guitar became our pastime and eventually our careers.

Fast forward back to 1987… with Bryan Ferry at the Buddokan in Japan. The show was going great, and one of my big solos was approaching. It was in a song called "In Every Dream Home a Heartache." The first four or five minutes are just Bryan and keyboards, but then the band kicks in big and loud for the solo. Well, the song is in E♭ and Doug handed me a guitar tuned to E. Oops. It was an extremely scary moment (for both of us) when I hit that first note! It was loud, and it was wrong. I recovered pretty quickly, but I was pretty mad, and there was a lot of shouting and cursing going on. I threatened to kill him; he told me to "f**k off" and threatened to quit. We were laughing about it by the end of the night. All in all, it was a great gig and a memorable night.

Since that tour, I've had the pleasure of having Doug at my side on many gigs. I really don't like doing gigs without him. Having a tech that knows his craft and knows your preferences and idiosyncrasies is indispensable. Doug is all of those things: a great guitar man and a great friend.

HOW DO YOU GET THAT JOB?
By Doug Redler

The Black Crowes were playing a five-night stand at the Nokia Theater in NYC. Since the first night was Halloween, the crew wanted to do some kind of prank. On this tour, the Crowes would play two sets, and in between there would be a quick change. In that short amount of time, the guys in the crew and I dressed up in Kiss costumes and played "Detroit Rock City." I was Ace Frehley, complete with a triple pickup cherry sunburst Les Paul. We thought it was funny, and the crowd seemed entertained, though I don't really think they understood what was going on. However, we hadn't told or asked the band in advance if it was cool for us to do this. Afterwards, Chris Robinson reprimanded us: "I'm glad you guys feel comfortable enough around us to do anything the f**k you want without asking." I think he was actually more upset that he didn't get to see us make fools of ourselves—not that we were disrespecting his authority! There is video of it out there somewhere on YouTube.

When I'm on the road, loading the band gear into a venue, setting up for a show, or stringing guitars, it's inevitable that someone will come up to me and ask, "Hey man, how do you get this job?" "Do you have to go to college?" "How did you learn how to fix that guitar?" "How did you get to work with that band?" "Have you seen Katy Perry naked?" Everyone seems to think my life must be amazing—traveling around the world, doing gigs, meeting "chicks," partying, and hanging out with famous rock stars.

It's not all fun and glamour. The travel is brutal whether you're in a tour bus, van, train, or plane. We live on a diet of coffee, candy, pizza, and beer. Weeks are spent away from loved ones, and I have missed holidays, births, weddings, and funerals. Being on a tour is mentally and physically challenging, and the hours are long. The road crew starts setting up for the show early in the morning, and by the end of the day, when all of the band gear, sound, and lights are packed back in the truck, most of the fans that attended are probably home and asleep. However, I have had the opportunity to work with musicians I idolized as a kid, have met many amazing people, and have traveled and made friends around the world.

It's one thing how I got the job, but it's another thing how I learned the job and how I kept the job. A lesson I learned on one of my first days on the road was, "Keep your mouth shut and your ears open," and I hope that I have abided by it. All the things you read and see in this book I have had to learn on my own over the years, and I've learned from my mistakes. Now, there are endless resources on the Internet and many guitar repair schools, but when I started touring, I had to do my own research. I got the Dan Erlewine books and videos and worked on my own guitars, the importance of the latter I cannot stress enough. I spent two months at Bryan Galloup's School of Guitar Building and was able to look over the shoulder of Scott Freilich at Top Shelf music in Buffalo, NY. I've also been fortunate to work with many great guitar technicians who were kind, patient, and willing to share their expertise, wisdom, tricks, and secrets. In fact, I still continue to pester Matt Brewster at 30th Street Guitars for answers.

Many friends over the years told me that I should write a book telling of my adventures on the road, though the initial idea came from a guitar repair class that I was teaching in NYC. The course was designed for musicians who were interested in doing their own guitar set-ups, repairs, and maintenance. I wanted to show them that quality work can be done at home with a few tools, practice, and patience. Now you have all that information and much more at your fingertips any time you need it. By following and practicing these basic steps, your guitar will play better, stay in tune, and sound great. In addition, you'll have the satisfaction of having done it all yourself and likely saved some money in the process.

CHAPTER 1:
Your Toolbox

Charlie Gillingham, the keyboard player from the Counting Crows, came to me during a gig with blood gushing out of his hand. During a gliss on his Hammond B-3 organ, one of the keys broke, slicing his finger to pieces. Not only did I have to patch him up to finish the show, I had to run out there, clean the keyboard, and reattach the key with glue. I had the type with an accelerator that cures in thirty seconds; by the next song, I had Gillingham and the keyboard back onstage.

Usually my biggest concern each day is to find a big enough place to set up my workbench, away from the lights and the sounds. Things fall out of the ceiling, and the venues are small so there isn't always enough room to work comfortably. I have to make my own "safe area" away from any obstacles or dangerous situations. Therefore, it's important for me to bring on the road everything I need because I do not have a workshop. I'm only able to bring what will fit in one or two cases, as I have to unpack, set everything up, and then put everything away every day. It's a long process, so I have to be efficient. My toolbox has evolved over the years as work cases have gotten smaller and as I refine my methods and my tools. But, as you can see from the story about the broken key, I have to be prepared for every unforeseen situation.

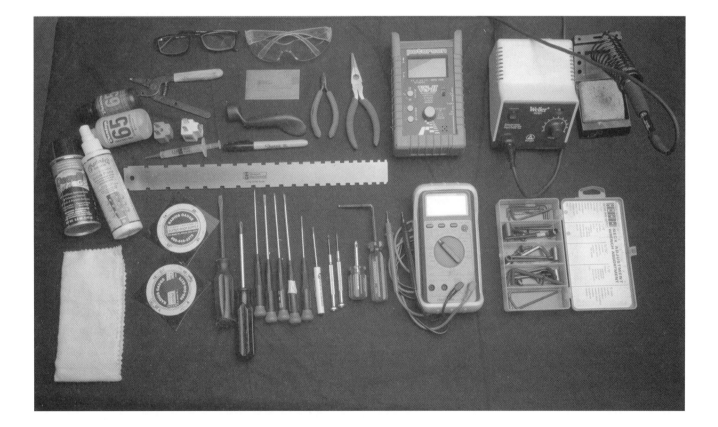

At this point, my toolbox contains the following. As we progress throughout the book, I'll get more specific about details regarding type, brand, sizes, etc.

Safety glasses
Assorted flat and Phillips head screwdrivers
Jeweler's screwdrivers
String winder
Wire clippers and strippers (the latter is the wire variety—not the alluring ones found after hours)
Peterson strobe tuner
Neck rest (for the guitar, not your head!)
Needle nose pliers
Assorted Allen wrenches
Long handled L-shaped Allen wrench for Martin guitars
Assorted socket wrenches (standard and metric)
Metal ruler (Stewart-MacDonald string action gauge)
Radius gauges
Small chisels and files
Various grades of sandpaper
Metal straightedge
Guitar polish and cleaning cloths
Lemon oil
Steel wool (extra fine 0000)
Nail file and clippers
Assortment of tape (gaffers, double-sided, painter's)
Wood glue and Super Glue
Sharpie
Toothpicks
Toothbrush
Q-Tips
Band-Aids
Sanding sticks (homemade)
Reading glasses (depending on one's age and to help reading the ruler!)
Digital multimeter
A good soldering iron (Weller WTCPT 60 temperature controlled soldering station)
A clean workbench (most important!)

You should know that you can purchase virtually everything you need for your toolbox already pre-packaged from Stewart-MacDonald (see Chapter 10). For example, they have a basic neck adjustment kit, which I purchased and have added to over the years. I learned from experience about having metric wrenches and now mark them with a piece of green tape so I can pick them out in a hurry. Make sure to have a soldering iron rather than a soldering gun. The gun can de-magnetize your pickups! The only time it can be useful is for removing frets because you can heat them up and just pull them out. But, yeah, guns are bad!

YOUR BRAND NEW BAG

I carry a "doctor's bag" with the basics, but my personal work box case for the Black Crowes is large, weighs 500 pounds, and includes virtually everything that could possibly be needed, like rivets and extra wheels for instrument cases. I have a powerful desk lamp, because if you don't have a good light, it doesn't matter where you are. A clip-on lamp is a good thing to have, too. Sometimes I work in very cold or hot temperatures, and you have no control over that. It doesn't help if you're sweating on a guitar when you are working over it, so I have a small, portable fan.

Out on the road, I can do pretty much everything except a complete fret job. However, I can file down a high fret or replace a nut, pickup, or damaged tuning machine—almost everything I could do in a guitar shop.

Tech Tip: Tape It or Glue It?

Gaffers tape used to be the go-to item for almost all band-related repairs. However, Super Glue may have superseded it. One time on a Dixie Chicks tour, guitarist Audley Freed cut his finger slicing bread, and I had to Super Glue it every day for two weeks so he could play.

CHAPTER 2:
Proper Stringing Techniques

As Jeff Thall describes in his foreword, my first tour was with Bryan Ferry in 1988, and there were a lot of songs in E♭. I only had two guitars to take care of, and they were Hamers that we had in exchange for an endorsement. One was tuned to standard pitch, and one was dropped a half step to E♭ so Jeff could play on a few songs in those keys. We were at the Buddokan in Japan, and it was Jeff's big solo in "Every Dream Home a Heartache." I handed him a guitar, he started playing, and then looked over at me and said, "I'm going to freakin' kill you!" The sound guy said, "He hit that first note, and I took him out of the mix." At that point, there was nothing you could really do. I had handed him the standard tuned guitar for his big solo in E♭, which would often go on for five to eight minutes. Fortunately, he was a good enough player to be able to transpose down a half step and get through it. It was very embarrassing and demoralizing for me, but Jeff laughed it off, and we still laugh about it to this day.

The first questions I ask when working on an artist's guitar are if and how often they want the strings changed, how they like their action, and if they mind if I clean the fretboard? Sometimes they like older strings that are not so bright—especially on an acoustic. But if an older string breaks during a show, I have to have a spare guitar ready or be able change that string really fast. Once Josh Grange (guitarist for kd Lang) had a string break on his pedal steel during a show—and that never happens. My hands were full, and Josh actually changed it himself during the next song. It's not easy on a guitar like that, especially when you have to stretch the strings a lot.

Tech Tip: Off with Their Heads!

I'm often asked if strings should be changed and replaced one at a time, or if they can be taken off all at once. My answer is what the late Cesar Diaz, the "Amp Doctor," said: "If the musician is there, I take them off one at a time. If not, (makes snipping noise), all at once!" However, with a Floyd Rose or a Bigsby whammy bar, you want to keep some tension on the bridge at all times to hold it in place. Therefore, changing them one at a time makes sense. I usually take the strings off two at a time unless the guitar fingerboard needs a good cleaning and polishing, at which time I will take all the strings off at once. That said, every time I change strings, I try to do some cleaning next to the frets with a cloth and scraper, because if the gunk builds up under there, it can eventually push up the frets. I also make sure to keep rosewood and ebony fingerboards lightly oiled, especially during the winter. Warning! Be careful taking coiled strings out of their envelopes or packs, as they can sometimes spring apart and hit you in the face!

STRINGING ALONG

Usually two or three wraps around a machine head post with the hole through the middle is sufficient for any big name guitarist. When I worked for Steve Stevens, he liked as many wraps as possible—all the way down to the metal nut at the bottom of the post—because he wanted a real sharp angle from the

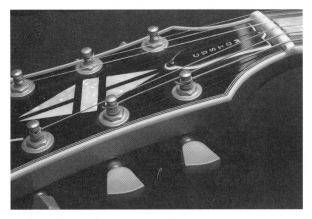

string nut to the bottom of the machine head post. He thought having more wraps and the steeper angle gave him a better sound. Some players think it is too much, and it was very difficult to get that many on. He also liked to have two or three inches of the string sticking out the other side of the post where I would normally clip it off. It was mostly for the look, but the length had to be pretty precise, and I would have to measure it every day. It was very dangerous to have those sharp ends sticking out, and I would stab myself every time I strung his guitars; I even had to get a tetanus shot! Plus, I had to be careful not to poke myself or somebody else in the eye! Apparently, it was part of Steve's look that matched his hair; what are you gonna do?

One time with Steve, while playing Virginia Beach, it was raining, and we were literally right on the beach. Between the salt air and the other elements, it really affected the guitars, and they sat in their cases for a couple of days before the next show. When I got them out, the strings were corroded, and I only had enough time to string three or four guitars before the sound check. On the ones I didn't re-string, I cleaned the best I could. Of course, those were the guitars Steve wanted for the sound check—Murphy's Law in action. These were the guitars with the Floyd Rose locking systems, and when I gave him one, he handed it right back to me and said, "Never, ever give me a guitar like this again." It was probably the most stern anyone has ever been with me. I couldn't say, "Hey man, here is what happened. I didn't have time to change them, etc." So I just said, "Okay" and bit my tongue.

Stringing a Tele

Push the string through the slot in the top of the post and cut it off about two or three posts past the one you are changing. That will leave enough slack for a sufficient number of wraps around the post after you put the cut end of the string straight down into the top of the post.

Step 1

Step 2

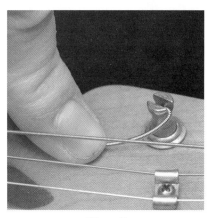

Step 3

Stringing a Les Paul or Strat

After pushing the string through the hole in the post, pull it back so you have about two inches of slack and follow the method for crimping and cutting off the excess string shown in the photos.

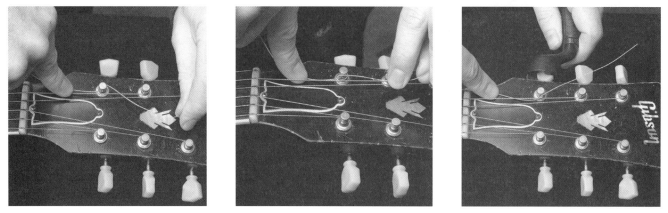

| Step 1 | Step 2 | Step 3 |

Stringing a Guitar with Sperzel or Other Locking Machine Heads

Pull the string all the way through with no slack, hand tighten the locking mechanism, and cut the string close to the post. There will be virtually no wraps around the post. When using locking tuners, always tune up past the desired pitch and then back down to it.

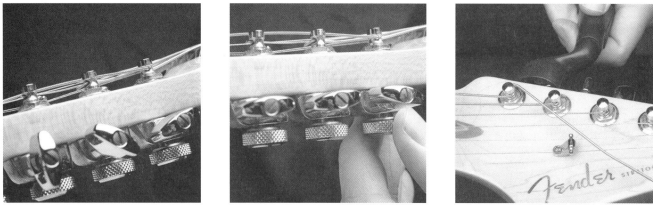

| Step 1 | Step 2 | Step 3 |

With Rich Robinson, we have so many guitars on the road because the band plays very long sets of three hours some nights. I string eight to ten guitars a day for a show. I used to wear out my arm and shoulder with a hand string winder, but eventually I wised up and got a string winder bit to put on the end of a drill. The reason I have to change his strings so much is because he uses a heavy brass slide that hits the frets and dents the strings; it just really beats them up. In addition, finger sweat and smoke in the clubs will wear strings out. After each show, I wipe down all the guitars to preserve the strings, which will give them a little more life for a few days. If a string breaks during a show, it's a disruption, which is never a good thing. Besides that, I don't always have time to change one during a Crowes concert because I'm concentrating on tuning guitars for the upcoming song. However, if it does happen, and Rich needs that guitar, I drop everything and get to it. I can have one restrung, stretched, and tuned in about a minute and ready for the next song.

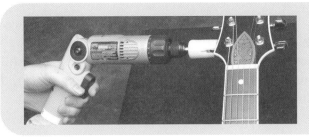

Tech Tip: Save Your Hands
Dean Markley makes a small, electric string winder that Guitar Center sells for around $20.

STRETCH IT TO THE LIMIT ONE MORE TIME

Stretching new strings is critical. After you restring your guitar, you need to give them a really good stretch up and down each string and then retune. Pulling up about one inch above the fingerboard should do it. You do not want to pull the string up too far and risk breaking it, but I stretch and retune as many as eight times to get them to settle in. If the guitar has a whammy bar, I'll stretch them by hand and with the whammy bar. If you test the tuning by raising or "dive bombing" with the bar and it stays at pitch, you know you're getting close. I'm not sure if it's possible to over-stretch strings, but I've never had it happen. Remember to always tune "low" to "high," string-wise, and to always tune "up" to pitch rather than "down."

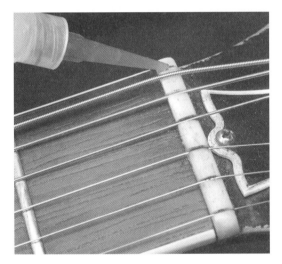

Also, the whole idea is to keep your guitar in tune when you play, so it is also important to always grease the nut when changing strings. There often seems to be a problem with the way a nut is cut. If a slot is too tight, there can be crinkling, or it can pull a string sharp or pinch when you bend a string. Big Bend's Nut Sauce or Planet Waves Lubricant both work well for that purpose. Also, lightly cleaning out the slots with very fine sandpaper (like #800 grit) before greasing will help prevent the string getting hung up in the slot. I clean out the nut slots on the road before every change of strings because dirt and gunk gets in there. A business card or a toothpick can do the trick, and more often than not I'll follow with the fine grit sandpaper.

Tech Tip: Use TLC
When changing strings, do not press them down into the nut slots any heavier than necessary to avoid undue wear.

BRAND PLACEMENT

Most players I know will notice a change in string gauges, but very few will know if I use a different brand of strings on their guitars. However, the type of string does matter more on acoustic guitars, and I have been trying to sneak in the coated strings without telling anybody. The coated strings do last longer and still have great tone. No one has noticed yet! The quality has been getting better and better over the years; Elixir, D'Addario, and Martin all make nice ones that I use. I change so many strings a week out on the road that if I can eliminate even a small percentage, it's well worth it. kd Lang will not let me change her strings. So I learned a trick from Paul Simon's tech: I "age" her strings. I keep a few packs out and exposed to the air under conditions on the road for a couple of weeks before I need them. But kd can still tell if there are new strings on her 1937 Gibson L-00 (named "Josephine"). She'll shoot me a look and say, "New strings?" Fortunately, we've never gotten to the point where she had them on so long that they started to break, which will happen with older strings depending on how hard a person plays and how much their hands sweat.

THE BRONZE AGE

Phosphor bronze is the standard for acoustics, though it is usually left up to me to make the choice. Everyone seems to like a brighter string, and phosphor bronze is brighter than bronze. Luther Dickinson from the North Mississippi Allstars, who now plays with the Crowes, tried DR brand phosphor bronze strings, and you could really hear the difference. However, what's more critical than the brand is how you string your guitar. Truthfully, there are many choices of strings now, and they are all good and reliable.

Tech Tip: Go on a Bender

When stringing acoustic guitars, I bend the ball end around my finger before placing it through the bridge and pushing it in with the bridge pin. The reason is that you want to make sure the ball end is hooked under the bridge plate. If it does not seat properly, besides causing tuning problems, the end of the string above the ball that is twisted can chew up the bridge plate, 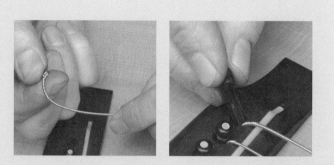 eventually causing an expensive repair. Likewise, with a Bigsby whammy bar, it's important to bend the string in the same place so it wraps itself tightly around the roller section of the bridge.

ELECTRIC AVENUE

"Vintage" electric strings with a high nickel content, stainless steel, and other alloys have been on the market, but no one has been that particular about that aspect with me. In fact, 99 percent of the players I work with use D'Addario XL electric .010s (.010–.046). Ernie Ball, Dean Markley, GHS, and Dunlop also make excellent electric strings.

Luther Dickinson is one of the few players I have worked with who uses a .009 set because he does these super-incredible bends. However, the heavier the string gauge, the easier it is to keep in tune. It's a real battle with .009s, especially when someone is using a whammy bar and bending the hell out of the strings, but Luther manages to stay in tune. A lot of that is due to stretching out new strings and his playing technique.

A plain G string can present tuning problems, no matter the gauge, as it is the largest of the three unwound strings. Recently, I've been making my guys put on a wound G—especially on guitars like an old Danelectro, where you cannot adjust the intonation due to the solid bridge design—and it helps noticeably.

The condition of the machine heads also affects tuning. Sometimes players want to keep their guitars as original as possible, including the machine heads. But they are such an important component in keeping a guitar in tune that if they start slipping because of worn gears, they should be replaced. (Note: If you replace vintage tuning machines, save the originals in case you ever want to sell the guitar and need to put them back on or at least provide them to the new owner.) New "vintage style" machine heads are available for those that want to maintain the vintage vibe.

Tech Tip: Up in Smoke

The plastic machine head buttons on vintage guitars, especially Gibsons from the '50s, were usually made from celluloid plastic that can spontaneously combust in a puff of smoke or deteriorate over time. If you see any evidence of cracking or shrinkage, it's a good idea to replace them immediately, as the fumes from the celluloid may tarnish and damage the metal parts and binding on the guitar.

While assessing the condition of the tuning machines, make sure that the screws that fasten them to the headstock are tight, as well as the nut that secures them at the bottom of the post. If they are Grover, Schaller, Gotoh, or other brands with an adjustment screw on the end of the button, they should be checked occasionally to make sure they are just tight enough to take up the slack as the gears inside will wear. Be sure not to make them too tight, as this can have the opposite effect and wear out the gears prematurely.

Tech Tip: Brother, Can You Spare a Tuner?

I was touring with Sam Phillips, who was married to T-Bone Burnett at the time. T-Bone was her guitar player, and Jerry Scheff (from Elvis Presley's band) was playing bass. It was an amazing band, and I got to hear some great Elvis stories from Jerry. Before a show, I was stringing T-Bone's vintage Kay "Jimmy Reed" model—his favorite guitar and the only guitar he had for the tour—and the plastic tuner knob on the machine head disintegrated in my string winder. I didn't have any spare tuners and ended up tying the string around the tuning post and using a wrench to turn the tuner, which was not cool! Now I always make sure to have spare tuners in my workbox, and you can also get just the vintage plastic knob of the tuner and replace it yourself if need be.

Around 2006, the Dixie Chicks were opening for the Eagles at the Nokia Theater in Los Angeles. At that time, I was taking care of the banjos for Emily Erwin Robinson, and there were a whole slew of them with wireless units. The sound man had a separate channel for each one. Tuning banjos is not one of my specialties, as I really don't like them. However, they've been following me around for most of my career. For the encore after a show that had gone really well, I realized I had given her the wrong banjo for the song with the wrong tuning; I was holding the one she should have had. So I started tuning the one I had with the idea of getting it out to her in time. I kept it connected to the wireless unit which the sound man had turned up, and the one she was playing was going through a channel that was turned down. I put a stick-on pickup on the headstock of the banjo to go into the tuner because it picks up the signal better, though the banjo itself was still plugged into the wireless unit. As the band played onstage, I was tuning the banjo, and it was coming out in the house because the sound man thought it was the one Emily was playing! Consequently, everyone heard the "ring ding ding ding" of me tuning the banjo. Eventually, the sound man figured out what happened, turned my banjo down, and turned hers up, but I was still clueless. After the show, everyone was coming offstage and giving me really dirty looks. I thought, "What's going on? It was a really great show." So I went to the production office, and the lighting guy said to me, "Nice solo."

CHAPTER 3:
Evaluating the Neck

I was at 30th Street Guitars in Manhattan one time with Rich Robinson because he needed another Strat. He had fallen in love with this white "Mary Kay" Strat that he had been playing a lot, and we needed another guitar as a backup. I found a 1972 Strat that was black, which would have been a custom color at that time. It was originally a sunburst, as could be seen on the upper bout where the finish had worn away from years of being rubbed. It was a really cool looking guitar, but it had been on the shelf for a while and did not play great. It needed frets, as the originals were really worn, and the neck was in an "up bow." Of course, Rich said, "I want to play it tonight," so we bought it. Matt Brewster did a quick grind and polish on the frets, and we took it to California. When we got there, I took the neck off and tightened the truss rod a few turns to straighten the neck, and Rich played it all night long.

A lot of times when we are on the road, the guys will go into guitar shops, find a guitar, bring it to soundcheck and say, "I want to play this tonight." Sometimes it's been sitting in the shop a long time, and you have no idea what has been done to the guitar, what parts have been replaced, or what work has been done. You don't know if the truss rod works or not, and you don't know what parts are original. The first thing you want to do when you are considering buying a used guitar is to evaluate the neck—starting with the condition of the truss rod. If it is stripped, and the nut (bolt) just keeps spinning, or is stuck and does not move at all, the guitar will be unplayable, necessitating an expensive neck replacement, as it is very difficult to repair truss rods. However, if it is in good working order, you are ready to proceed with either maintaining or restoring the good health of your new neck!

Tech Tip: Gauge Yourself
Radically changing string gauges to either heavier or lighter strings will require a truss rod adjustment, as will most likely the change of seasons or climate because of a change in humidity. One or the other (or both) will change the whole dynamic of the guitar.

NECKING
Next, make sure the guitar is tuned to pitch with the string gauge you plan on using and check for the proper neck adjustment. The easiest and quickest way to do that is by "sighting the neck." Hold the guitar so that you're looking down from the headstock along the top edge of the neck on the bass side where the frets end. Then turn the guitar upside down and sight down the treble side as well. You want to look for an "up bow," a "back bow," humps (especially around where the neck joins the body), high frets, or even loose frets on an older instrument.

Another way to evaluate the neck is with a straightedge placed along the frets and by observing the amount of space, or bow, between it and the frets around the middle of the neck. Stewart-MacDonald makes a "notched" straightedge specifically for this purpose (the notches fit over the frets) so you can see exactly the distance between the straightedge and the fingerboard.

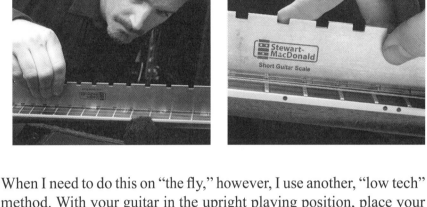

When I need to do this on "the fly," however, I use another, "low tech" method. With your guitar in the upright playing position, place your right hand thumb on the low E string directly on the fret wire itself where the neck joins the body (usually at fret 15, 17, or 19) and your left hand index finger directly on fret 1. In essence, you're creating a straightedge with the string itself. Then, with either your left hand pinky or right hand index finger—whichever one you can stretch the furthest—use the "tapping method" to lightly tap the low E string around frets 5–7 to make sure there is some space, or relief, under the string. A good "rule of thumb" (pun intended!) is there should be a space between the string and the frets that is approximately the thickness of a business card. If there is no space at all, and the

low E string is actually touching the frets around the middle of the neck, then you need to loosen the truss rod in order to allow the pull of the strings to create a small amount of bow, or relief, in the neck.

I was constantly adjusting necks for the B-52s. They had different guitars for every song, every guitar was in a different tuning, and some guitars only had five strings—like the Tele for "Rock Lobster," for instance. The low E string was tuned down to C—a .060 string was used so it wouldn't be too flabby—and it was missing the G string in order to accommodate the rhythm part. As soon as I put that .060 on and brought it up to pitch, the neck went into an up bow. The heaviest bass string that had previously been on the guitar was likely only a .046. All I could do was tighten the hell out of the truss rod to straighten out the neck.

TAKE A BOW

I believe guitars play best with some bow. Remember, you should be able to see some light between the edge of the notched straightedge and the fingerboard, or between a regular straightedge and approximately frets 5–7, for example. I do like to have the strings as low as possible, as it helps intonation and playability, but there always needs to be some relief under the strings. Keep in mind that "as low as possible" is a relative term and that all guitars, even ones of the same model and year of manufacture, are different. You never want the action so low that it inhibits string vibration and hinders a clear, clean, sustained sound. Actually, there is a whole science about string vibration that is beyond the scope of this book, but it may be worth your while to investigate at the library (old school) or online.

RATTLE AND HUM

If your strings rattle or buzz, the action (string height) is either too low or you have a "back bow," which would be obvious when using a straightedge or even just sighting along the edge of the neck. A back bow means that the neck curves up under the strings instead of away from the strings and is the result of the truss rod being too tight, thereby providing too much counterforce to the pull of the strings.

Tech Tip: Bend Over

While either too much relief or a back bow is to be avoided for the best playability, too much relief is desirable as opposed to a back bow that will result in the "fretting out" of various notes. Many old time guitarists, especially of the blues variety, often played great on very high action due in part to excessive bow. However, no modern guitarist should have to suffer such an indignity with all other aspects of good neck "health" being equal.

There are several reasons for not having your strings too low. Besides buzzing, it will hinder string bending, as it makes it difficult to dig in with your fingers and get a good grip. It's better to have the action medium to medium high and therefore avoiding your fingers slipping off the strings when bending 2 1/2 steps like Albert King! However, if your strings are too high, the action will feel mushy, making it hard to play fast and cleanly. We'll address action height in more detail in Chapter 4.

When you tighten the truss rod, you make the neck straighter and lower the action, making it easier to play. As a result, the guitar plays more in tune since the strings have less distance to travel to the frets.

Tech Tip: Not a Haiku

A good mnemonic to remember for which way to turn the nut on the truss rod is "Righty tighty, lefty loosey."

GIMME BACK MY BULLETS

Though opinion is divided on the aesthetics, Fender guitars with the "bullet," or recessed, truss rod are far easier to access than the one on vintage guitars, which are at the butt end of the neck and partially hidden by the pickguard. The latter is a pain in the ass to adjust, as the strings must be loosened as well as the pickguard, which needs to be slid out of the way. However, a good trick that I learned is to apply a capo at the first fret so that when you loosen the strings, it holds them in place for tuning them back up with less bother. This method of clamping the strings in place also works very well should you need to take the neck off the body for adjusting the truss rod, which is a last resort. In that case, you need to make sure the strings have little or no tension, and the four bolts and plate that fasten the neck to the body must be removed.

Tech Tip: Fender Neck-Checking

Be extremely careful whenever removing or replacing the neck on a Fender Strat or Tele so as to not chip the paint or lacquer around the neck cavity. You'll notice on older Strats, particularly, that there are often chips around the edge of the cavity where the neck was forcefully jammed into place instead of being put back in slowly and gently. Also be aware that you may need to place a shim between the neck and the floor of the cavity if the bridge pieces are as low as they can go and the action is still too high. Warning: If the Allen screws are sticking up way above the bridge piece, and you find your palm getting scratched when strumming close to the bridge and muting, that's a clear sign that the neck needs to be shimmed so the bridge pieces can be raised back up! A piece of plastic credit card will work well for this purpose, or even a guitar pick.

I am constantly adjusting the necks on guitars for touring musicians. The weather changes, guys are changing string gauges, and after they are out on the road building up their chops, they want their action changed. These days, many guitars are not made as well as they used to be; the wood is a little softer, for example. The point is that you need to be aware that truss rod adjustments are a part of regular guitar maintenance. You should learn how to do the basics and be prepared to apply them on occasion. You also need to know when the neck condition requires the attention of a professional: if it's twisted, if tightening the truss rod does not straighten it, or if the truss rod is literally broken because the nut just keeps turning with no affect.

Tech Tip: Don't Fret

Fret replacement or even a "grind and polish," which is the occasional leveling of all the frets with a smooth, flat grinding stone in order to have your guitar play in tune all over, is beyond the scope of this book. However, with the strings off, it's very important to wipe and clean the frets (see Chapter 1) with Gorgomyte or 0000 steel wool to remove the burrs that occur over time from playing. Be sure to use masking tape to cover the pickups so that the metallic filings do not get attracted to them. Also, on Fender-type maple fingerboards (as opposed to rosewood or ebony as on Gibson guitars, for example), you'll need to mask off the wood in between the frets to avoid scratching the varnish. It's necessary to clean out the gook that builds up from your hands along the edge and even under the frets, or else the wood could eventually rot underneath. As a further precaution, you should always wipe down your strings every time after playing, to increase string life and help keep the neck clean.

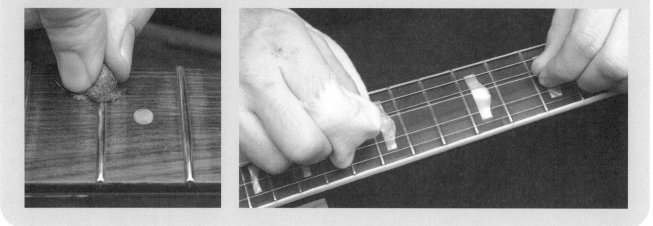

Remember that for a lot of adjustments there are no set rules. Get the adjustments to where you like your guitar to play. When I start working for someone, and they have a guitar they really like, I always take measurements at fret 15 on the two E strings and make note of the action by using the "tapping method" at fret 5. Before I make any adjustments, I take into account the player's style and how the guitar is set up at that moment. I'll then try to match that on his or her other guitars. Some like the neck as straight as possible. Rich Robinson has a white reissue Gibson SG that he loves and wants all his guitars to play the way it does, so I have taken my measurements and made notes of all the important factors relating to its neck adjustment. It's important for me to know what my clients want in the way of playability. Just because I like my guitars to play a certain way does not mean they will want the same.

ACOUSTICALLY SPEAKING

Generally, there's not much you can or perhaps should do to the action on an acoustic once it's set to factory specs. However, sometimes it is necessary to either lower or raise the saddle due to the change of seasons regarding humidity. For the former, this just involves sanding the bottom of the saddle with a fine grit paper. Be sure to only take a little off at a time, reinserting it into the bridge and retuning until you bring the action down to where you want it. It's very important to sand evenly, so use a sanding block or lay the sandpaper on a table and move the saddle back and forth on top of it. If the action is too low, you can make a shim from a business card or an old credit card and cut it to fit along the bottom of the saddle. A little Elmer's glue will hold it in place nicely. Be aware that these adjustments, either way, will only need to be slight in order to restore the action back to your preference.

Tech Tip: Check the Oil, No Gas

Before I clean and oil a fretboard I always check with the guitar's owner to be sure they want the fretboard cleaned. Many musicians like the accumulation of dirt and oil on the fretboard and on the neck of the guitar. They feel there is a special "mojo" in all of that gunk. However, I feel it is important to clean the fretboard regularly to extend its life, as dirt can be abrasive over time on the surface of the fingerboard. I do it every time I change strings.

Oiling the fretboard only needs to be done once or twice a year. By conditioning the fretboard you can stop it from drying out and cracking, as well as preventing the frets from coming loose. Conditioning the fretboard will also make it look great and bring out the grain in the wood. There are many different oils to choose from, though most are just mineral oil with lemon scent such as Planet Waves, Dunlop, and Dr. Ducks Ax Wax, to name a few. A little goes a long way and one bottle should last forever. **Warning:** Only use oil on rosewood and ebony fretboards as generally found on Gibson, Epiphone, PRS, Gretsch, and Guild guitars, for example, or on other unfinished woods. *Never* use oil on a maple fingerboard Fender Strat or Tele, or other guitars with finished fretboards.

First, I remove the strings and always oil the fretboard *after* I polish the frets. On a really dirty fretboard, I will scrape the sides of the frets with a radius gauge where they meet the wood, being careful not to scratch the varnish on finished fretboards. The pointed edges of the radius gauge can get deep in between the fret and the fretboard and dig out lots of the grime. Gorgomyte and 0000 steel wool are good for cleaning frets as well. Then I will use Parma Fretboard Cleaning solvent to get rid of the rest of the gunk, at which point you are essentially done on finished fingerboards

 except for wiping clean with paper towels and lightly buffing with a soft, lint-free cloth. Once the unfinished fretboard is dry, I just use a very small amount of lemon oil. I apply it with a paper towel, let it absorb for about 5–10 minutes and remove the excess with buffing pads that I get from Grizzly Industrial Supply. Be sure the oil has completely been absorbed before re-stringing the guitar.

CHAPTER 4:
Setting the Action

So far in this book, we've put strings on the guitar, adjusted the truss rod, and straightened the neck. The next thing we want to address regarding playability is string height followed by intonation, as the latter is always the last thing you want to do on a guitar.

Tech Tip: Watch the Curves

On Fender bridges with individual saddles that adjust for height, it's important that the radius, or the curvature of the bridge saddles, match the radius of the fingerboard at the butt end of the neck. If not, you are liable to get buzzing. On Gibson Tune-o-matic type bridges, this is only possible to a very small degree by filing, as the individual saddles may only be adjusted back and forth (front to back) for intonation and not up and down for action. Of course, it's also a personal preference if you want your action a little higher or a little lower—or, for you blues busters, if you want just the top three treble strings to be slightly higher above the radius to facilitate string bending. However, there is the law of diminishing returns. If the strings are set too high, intonation problems can occur because the strings will go slightly sharp when pressed to the frets, despite ease of bending and clearer tone.

TOOLING ALONG

There are three tools that I use for setting the action: a good metal ruler (I like the string action gauge that you can get at Stewart-MacDonald), a cheap pair of glasses, (as the measurements we use are either in 32nds or 64ths—it is that precise!), and a really good light to work under. If I do a Strat, for instance, the matching Allen wrenches that fit the screws on the bridge saddles will also be necessary. Classic Tele bridges with the three brass barrels, as opposed to the modern designs that are similar to a Strat, only require a small slotted screwdriver, as does a Tune-o-matic-type bridge.

Another good tool to have is a radius gauge from Stewart-MacDonald. It's a little piece of cardboard with four sides that you place over the fingerboard to measure the radius of your neck. Then you can bring it over to a Fender bridge and raise the saddles until they match the particular radius for that guitar.

On a Tune-o-matic bridge, it's harder to do because it only has a slight arc, but it is still really important to have the radius correct. I was working on Rich Robinson's 1963 Gibson ES-335 one time, and we realized that some of the strings were higher than others on the bridge. A lot of it was from wear, because he plays very hard, so some of the saddles on the middle strings had their slots worn too deep. Instead of replacing the entire bridge, which I did not want to do, I filed the slots deeper on the two E strings to get it back to the proper radius with the middle four strings and then raised the bridge on both sides to bring it back to where the action was originally.

In more extreme cases of wear to the saddles, it may be necessary to replace them individually or with a whole new bridge, which will be stronger and easier to adjust. TonePros makes a good product. In either case, you'll need to cut the string slots on new saddles, which will require a set of very fine files, such as jeweler's files.

Tech Tip: Stringing Along

When cutting new saddle slots, be sure to always leave the strings on your guitar (albeit slackened and pulled to the sides of the neck) so that you can keep checking your work by placing the string in the new slot and tuning it back up near pitch.

Have your ruler handy when you are filing saddle slots so that you can continuously check your action height at the 15th fret. The radius gauge helps through this procedure as well, so I combine them both. I probably use the ruler 99 percent of the time, but the radius gauge is important so that you know the exact radius of the neck and can match it on the bridge.

Tech Tip: Strings Without Wires

On an acoustic guitar, there's no room for error or deviation when building the saddle because it must match the neck radius, and that is where the radius gauge really comes into play. What you do is take the radius of the neck with the gauge, trace it onto the saddle blank, and then sand it down. Of course, then you have to compensate for the B string, which is called the "B-bump," if anyone is interested. (See Chapter 9 for more.)

Tech Tip: Bridges with Troubles

Gibson Tune-o-matic bridges have been made in several varieties since their introduction on the Les Paul Custom in 1954. The original, or "standard," is referred to as the BR-010 or "ABR-1." It's considerably thinner (from front to back) than subsequent models, has slim, threaded posts that go right into the top of the guitar, uses inconvenient thumbwheels to raise and lower the action, and contains a fragile piece of retaining wire to hold the saddles in place. The "Modern Tune-o-matic" is thicker, has a threaded pot inserted into the top of the guitar with slot-head posts inside for far easier adjustments, and no retaining wire. The "Refined Standard Tune-o-matic" has slimmer threaded pots while maintaining posts with the screwdriver adjustment. There is also the later and clunky BR-030 "Nashville" model, which is much thicker and heavier than any of the others, providing for more intonation adjustment on the saddles. Be aware that, except for the latter, the standard Tune-o-matic bridges tend to slowly collapse over time, particularly if string sets heavier than .010 are used.

Fender, Gibson, Martin, etc., all have "factory specs" regarding the string height at which they set their instruments prior to sending them out to the dealers. It's usually between three and four 64ths of an inch for all six strings following the radius of the fingerboard at fret 15.

On a Strat, I usually begin low with a height of 2/32" or even 2/64" as measured at fret 15 for each string. (Some guitar techs measure at fret 12, and some at fret 17 as well.) I like to begin with the low E string. Though I do start with a lower measurement, I usually find that the factory specs are where I want to eventually be, as you can often get buzz on the G, B, and high E strings if they are below those measurements. However, I've found 3/64" or 4/64" across the board to be the "sweet spot." Most players I work with love it at that setting. As mentioned previously in Chapter 3, when I find a measurement that somebody likes, I write it down. That way, should an artist come up to me and say, "This guitar is different; something doesn't feel right," I can go back to my notes, get out a ruler and respond, "Here is where we started, and here is where you liked it." Unfortunately, I run into that problem a lot. I will get the action where I really like it, and it's playing well, and then the artist will pick up his guitar, and it will be "fretting out" on one note at one fret. So I'll find I have to raise it a bit and compromise.

Most guitars are not perfect. Of course, I know if something has gone awry, because I can see if the action has come up—usually from climate change making the neck move. Necks do move up and down, especially when string gauges are changed. Remember, if you find you have to raise your strings more than 4/64" or 5/64" to remove buzzing, there's a problem somewhere else. It could be a high fret, for example, especially if the buzzing occurs around the frets 12–17 where the neck meets the body and there is sometimes a hump.

Tech Tip: Block the Block

Before setting action height on a Strat with a whammy bar, it's important to make sure the bridge assembly is sitting flush on the top of the guitar. You don't want it angled up or down, as is usually done to facilitate "dive bombs" or vigorous mechanical string bending/vibrato. One way to accomplish this is to screw down the springs that connect to the steel "inertia block" (under the plastic cover on the back of the guitar) until the metal plate they are attached to touches the front wall of the cavity. However, what I do is get a little block of wood and put it between the body cavity on the back of the guitar and the steel inertia block. Make sure the string tension is slack, so that the bridge assembly may be easily pushed flush to the top before the wood block is inserted. By the way, there's an ongoing argument about whether a Strat with a whammy bar has more sustain than a "hard tail" Strat, or vice versa. There is some opinion that a whammy bar Strat has more sustain because of the mass of the inertia block which was initially designed to help counteract the pull of the strings on the bridge assembly. However, there are many other things that affect sustain, such as a new nut. If you have a guitar that does not "ring" and feels dead, try putting a new nut on it; it could start ringing again. There are also those who believe that brass hardware will increase sustain and perhaps create a brighter tone. In the '80s, people swore by graphite nuts, but I always prefer a bone nut.

STOP IT!

On a Gibson Les Paul, 335, SG, or similar instrument, the stop tailpiece behind the Tune-o-matic bridge should be lowered to the point where there is the tiniest space between the strings and the back edge of the bridge. Though having the "break over angle" as steep as possible is desirable for tone and sustain, if the strings touch the back edge of the bridge on their way to the stop tailpiece, intonation problems and buzzing will be likely. However, if the bridge and consequently the action, are low enough that the stop tailpiece may be screwed down flush and tight to the top, a noticeable increase in sustain should result.

Tech Tip: Don't Ask, Don't Tell

There used to be a sign in Matt Umanov Guitars on Bleecker Street in Greenwich Village, NY that stated: "Do not ask to have your action as low as possible without buzzing." However, the straighter the guitar neck is, the better it will play and the more it will play in tune. The trade-off to this is that there will be more fret buzz, and you will have less volume since the strings are so low against the fretboard. The more relief the neck has, the harder it is to play, though there will be less buzzes and more volume. It will also have more intonation problems since the strings are higher and will tend to get bent or pulled sharp in pitch.

TALE OF THE SCALE

Scale length is the distance from the nut to the saddle. Theoretically, the 12th fret should be exactly half way. Gibson uses a shorter scale length than Fender and Martin, which results in less string tension and a guitar that is generally easier to play—especially as regards string bending. However, some people feel that the longer scale length on the Strat makes barre chords and other voicings up the neck sound clearer and more defined. This seems to be most apparent when playing Jimi Hendrix-style chord melody as on "Little Wing," for instance.

LEARN TO COMPENSATE

Intonating your guitar follows setting the action height and involves moving the individual bridge saddles on electric guitars (or acoustics with moveable bridge pieces) either towards the fingerboard or back towards the butt end of the instrument. When you adjust intonation, you're compensating for the sharpness that occurs when pressing the strings to the frets so that the guitar plays in tune all up and down the neck. What you are going to do is either lengthen (make flat) or shorten (make sharp) the string length via the adjustment screws at the bridge.

Tech Tip: Name That Tune

Understand that having a fretted instrument play in tune up and down the neck in all keys is a theory that, in reality, ends up being a compromise. A modern system of scientific fret placement and bridge design that comes closest is the "Buzz Feiten Tuning System" designed by guitarist Buzz Feiten.

Though being in tune in all keys and at all fret positions is a compromise, no one wants to hear it. I can't get away with it. So, sometimes I'll watch where a guitarist plays most frequently on the neck and then tune for that chord—a C, for example. Or, if they play around the fifth position, I'll intonate so that the guitar plays best in tune at that location. For kd Lang, I always tune her B string by fretting it at the 12th fret because, for some reason, she always hears that note as being flat. For others, it's the A note at the 2nd fret on the G string where I'll tune it to A rather than open G. If a player says to me, "My guitar is out of tune here," then I have to figure out a way to fix it. Some like their G string slightly sharp because it sounds better to their ears. A perhaps apocryphal story about John Lennon with the Beatles tells of him slightly de-tuning his G string, the reason being that he wanted his aunt to be able to tell which guitar was his on the recordings.

As when evaluating the neck, you want to have your guitar in the playing position and you need to use a good strobe tuner. I recommend the Peterson, which is about $600, or the Peterson virtual strobe tuner, which costs much less.

1. Pluck the string open with your thumb or finger (not a pick) and tune to pitch
2. Fret and pluck the note at fret 12 (the octave)
3. If the fretted note is sharp compared to the open string, lengthen the string until the open string and fretted note match exactly.
4. If the fretted note is flat, shorten the string until they match.

Unless your intonation is way off to begin with, or you have made a radical change in string gauges, these adjustments will be minute and incremental. Sometimes you can run out of adjustment in either direction, particularly on the old style Tune-o-matic bridges, and especially for the G string, which is problematic anyway because it is usually a large plain string.

The vintage Tele bridges consisting of three brass barrels with two strings on each are great for tone, and I hate to replace them, but they can present intonation problems. There are several good replacements, such as from Callaham in Virginia, that keep the three saddles. They're made from heavier brass so they really ring out and, more importantly, they're angled for compensation. They stay in tune and are very easy to use. When intonating this type of bridge, I get the G and the B in tune first, since they are the hardest, and the D and the high E that share the saddles, respectively, will usually follow.

Tech Tip: Plain Janes

Be aware that the plain G, B, and E strings on any guitar may need more compensation. I don't want to call it cheating, but they may need to be made slightly longer (flatter). By the way, using a wound G will go a long ways to solving intonation problems. I try to get my guys to use them, and they will complain and complain until I put one on their guitar and say, "Play it! Look, it's in tune." But it's still a hard sell.

TIME FOR A CHANGE

The two questions I am asked the most are, "How many guitars do you restring a day, and how often should strings be changed?" With the Crowes, we take 30 guitars on the road, and I string eight to 10 a day. On days off, I often spend my time in hotel rooms stringing guitars in order to stay ahead. Rich Robinson plays so many guitars that I do not have to change strings on each one before every show, except on his main ones. He tends to like the sound of new strings, and changing them so often prevents breakage. He uses guitars with 11 different tunings, so I have a backup for each one and am able to rotate them. With kd Lang, I only change one or two a day because her band doesn't play as long or as hard. Some players have "toxic sweat," and after one show their strings will be all dented from the frets and nasty.

There are other things to look for when considering changing strings besides the dents. You also want to check for rust or oxidation. Whenever I get a guitar back during a show, I always wipe off the strings, in between songs if I can. I always wipe them off after a show as well before I put them back in the case. Keeping the strings clean will extend their life. Finger-ease helps, too, and you can get another day or two out of heavily played strings. One of my tricks for making the strings feel like new instead of always changing them (that I do not tell the guys!) is Dunlop Ultraglide 65 String Cleaner & Conditioner, which is excellent for taking off all the crap. In addition, it can be used for guitars that have been sitting around for a while. I use it on mine when I am away from home on the road for extended periods of time.

Keep in mind that the main reason for changing strings on the road is to keep them from breaking. I left the Crowes at one point, and another guitar tech filled in. When I returned, Rich said to me, "I hate these strings; they are always breaking." I replied, "We used that brand of strings for two years, and you never had any break." When I was away from the band, they just didn't know that I was changing them so frequently.

Acoustic guitars are different. k.d. hates for me to change her acoustic strings, and sound guys do too, as it makes the guitar so much brighter than it was with the old strings. She likes them to be so dead that it gets to the point where you cannot even tune them anymore. My trick is to leave acoustics with new strings out for a while so they age and get some hand grease on them. My experience is that musicians and sound men like acoustic strings better with some of the "shine" off.

CHAPTER 5:
Adjusting the Pickups

On one of my first days on the job with Jeff Thall backing Bryan Ferry, he came in with a bag of pickups and said, "Put these on all my guitars." I knew nothing about soldering, and I replied, "What, are you crazy?" To that he said, "You gotta learn sometime." So he kind of threw me into it by just saying, "Do it." Luckily, there were schematics for me to follow, and now it's even easier to find them on the Internet. With pickup replacement, sometimes it's just a matter of following the wires from one to another.

As we all know, the search for perfect tone is never ending. Most players go through different pickups, and many of us destroyed good '60s and '70s Strats and Jazzmasters by replacing the weaker single coil pickups with more powerful humbuckers.

Tech Tip: The Eternal Debate

There are pros and cons to both Fender-style single coil pickups and Gibson-style humbucking pickups. Obviously, the biggest drawback to single coil pickups is their susceptibility to unwanted noise or the "RF" (radio frequency) factor. The use of high gain amps and stomp boxes only makes the problem worse. At large concerts, you have tons of lights, video projections, and all sorts of interference like taxi dispatchers and radios, all of which your Strat through a tube Fender Deluxe may receive and amplify. There are gigs where a guitar player with single coil pickups will have to put an "X" on the stage with tape to mark the spot where he can stand without interference. The big plus for guitars with humbucking pickups is that they "buck the hum" and filter out the unwanted "RF" and other extraneous signals flying through the air. But, you're not going to tell David Gilmour not to play his Strats, so his techs may have put some sort of shielding around his pickups or resorted to other tricks to minimize the problem. You may also want to try stacked humbuckers in a Strat or Tele, though the sound will change and may not be to your liking. Many companies, like Lindy Fralin, make a variety of replacement pickups for single coil Fender guitars.

There's a music venue in Minneapolis called First Avenue that is owned by Prince. All the lighting dimmers are under the stage. If you have a Marshall or other high gain amp and you want to play a Strat, it's going to buzz all night long. So you have to ride your volume control constantly, rolling it off when not playing, to solve the noise problem. When you're playing, generally the amplified strings will drown out the RF. Alternatively, you can switch to a humbucking guitar for a particularly troublesome gig.

FEEL THE PULL

A pickup is simply an electromagnet consisting of thousands of coils of thin copper wire wrapped around a bobbin. It turns string vibration into electrical current, which is then transferred to an amplifier where the relatively weak signal is increased in volume many times over. The closer the pickup is to the strings, the louder and stronger the signal. Single coil pickups as found on Strats and Teles have roughly half the output of humbucking pickups, though Gibson P-90 pickups have more than standard Fender pickups. In addition, classic Fender single coil pickups do not have adjustable pole pieces (magnets) as found on humbuckers and Gibson P-90 pickups.

A GOOD PICKUP LINE

Understand that on a multi-pickup guitar with the same pickups in each position and at the same distance below the strings, the pickup closest to the fingerboard will sound darker and louder than the one closest to the bridge. This is due to the fact that the string vibrates longer and slower as you move away from the bridge, and shorter and quicker near the bridge. The slower the vibration, the lower the pitch or frequency, and vice versa. This phenomenon can be heard on an electric guitar with the volume off or on an acoustic guitar, as well.

Rich Robinson will come up to me all night long at a gig saying, "Raise my pickups, raise my pickups!" When adjusting your pickups in relation to their proximity to the strings, it's important to listen to the sound of the strings carefully on both sides of the pickup in order to balance the bass and treble response to your taste, along with the sustain, which is also affected. What I basically do at first when adjusting an artist's pickups is to make sure that the strings are not touching the pickups (or pole pieces on the pickups) when pressing the strings at the highest fret. On a Strat, I leave 1/16" on the treble side for all three pickups

and 1/8" on the bass side. However, what I then do is to set the bridge pickup first, the middle pickup a little higher, and then the bridge pickup a bit higher than the middle pickup. The reason is to shoot for a balance between each pickup by compensating for the louder volume as you move towards the fingerboard.

Tech Tip: Proper Screwing

When using a screwdriver, always place your left thumb and index finger around the tip of the screwdriver. This will prevent the screwdriver from slipping and causing irreparable damage to your guitar finish. It's also a good "rule of thumb" to never hold or hand anything over your guitar while you are working on it. If something drops on your guitar, the results can be disastrous.

Some players like to have the pickup they use for most of the soloing to be louder than the one they use for rhythm. That way, they use their amp for gain and get a natural boost when they switch between pickups without touching their volume control or stepping on a distortion/overdrive box. It's a method worth considering. However, if you also use a stomp box regularly for soloing, it may produce too great a jump in volume over the other instruments. That said, you cannot beat the sound of a Strat straight into a vintage Fender Vibrolux! Many players like to get the most power and tone from their guitar via the pickups, then the amp, and lastly the stomp box in the signal chain.

Tech Tip: What Do You Have to Gain?

"Gain" refers to the amount of overdrive or distortion, as opposed to volume, which refers to loudness. You will notice that some amps have channels or controls labeled "Gain," "Drive," or "Master Volume," which affect distortion, in addition to "Volume" for overall level.

BUCKING THE HUM

With Gibson-type humbucking pickups on a Les Paul, ES-335, or SG, for example, it's necessary to adjust the height of the pole pieces (magnetized slot head screws) as well as the entire unit. I like to start with

the pole pieces flush to the top of the pickup covers. I then use the radius gauge as a guide, because you want them to match the curvature of the strings. The initial goal is always to have a balanced sound from string to string, along with between pickups. Consequently, the pole pieces underneath the two E strings may end up remaining flush with the top of the covers. After that, I raise the entire pickup unit so that I have 3/32" above the pole pieces of the neck pickup when the strings are pressed at the last fret. On the bridge pickup, the measurement will be 1/32" to compensate for the perceived louder volume of the neck pickup. Keep in mind that these are merely suggested measurements. However, make sure that no string is touching a pole piece when pressing down at the highest fret. Using your ears always works best for this. Arpeggiate a chord and listen to be sure your volume is consistent from the high to low strings.

Tech Tip: Play All the Angles

For maximum performance on pickups with adjustable pole pieces, always make sure the slots in the screws are turned at a diagonal under the strings—not parallel or at right angles to the strings.

Some people have experimented with humbucking pickups by dropping the entire unit flush with the top of the guitar (or even below) and then turning the pole pieces out much farther than usual for what they perceive as a brighter, sharper, single coil-type effect. Others also try the opposite method of screwing the pole pieces down flush with (or even below) the top of the covers and then raising the whole unit up so that the covers are very close to the strings for a rounder, darker sound.

Many guitarists like the look and think it enhances the sound to remove the pickup covers from humbuckers. However, the covers are there for shielding and to protect the ultra-thin copper wiring on the bobbin from being physically damaged. Therefore, I do not recommend it.

Tech Tip: Green with Envy

Legendary Fleetwood Mac guitarist Peter Green was once in a car accident with his iconic 1957 sunburst Les Paul Standard. The repairman who fixed it accidentally wrapped the wire coil around the bobbin of the neck pickup in reverse, resulting in a funky, out-of-phase sound when the selector switch was in the middle position with both pickups on. Another way to accomplish the same result is to reverse the magnet in the pickup so that the "north" and "south" poles point in the opposite direction. Be aware that the tone of the neck pickup or bridge pickup alone will not be affected. Green also had the entire neck pickup turned around so that the pole pieces were closer to the bridge pickup instead of the neck, though this did not seem to alter his sound noticeably.

THE GIBSON P-90 PICKUP

Gibson P-90 single coil pickups are almost as powerful as humbuckers and come in two varieties. The older style, which is often (but not always) found on hollow body Gibson guitars, attach directly to the top of the instrument and have adjustable pole pieces (magnetized slot head screws). The relatively newer version, as found on the pre-1957 Les Paul and some SGs, have adjustable pole pieces through a unit that may be raised and lowered in the top of the solid body instruments. They seem to be identical in sound and output except for the difference allowed in adjustment. Gibson has

also produced a P-100 that is a stacked humbucker designed to combat the hum associated with virtually all single coil pickups, but I do not recommend them, as they lack the bite of a standard, classic P-90 that is prized by so many players.

Tech Tip: Another Phase

The wire leads on a guitar equipped with two P-90 pickups may be reversed on the neck pickup to also achieve a very cool "out-of-phase" sound. It is my opinion that the middle position on most two-pickup Gibsons, be they humbuckers or single coils, lack character and are only good for tuning!

CHAPTER 6:
Basic Bass Guitar Set-up

Setting up a bass for top performance is similar to setting up a guitar, just with a few other things to think about; as it turns out, size does matter! For example, due to the heavier string gauges, larger frets, and longer scale, bass action needs to be relatively higher than on a guitar.

GETTING SOME ACTION

Using the truss rod adjustment, make the neck as straight as possible and then add some relief by backing off (counter-clockwise) on the truss rod tension. The amount of relief should be approximately double that of a guitar (the thickness of two business cards), though every instrument will have its own optimum amount to be determined.

> **Tech Tip: Don't Fret**
> Fretless bass necks should be adjusted as straight as possible, as there is no danger of fret buzz or rattle.

First, tune to pitch. Next, check the bridge pieces to make sure they follow the curvature of the fingerboard. Then, either raise or lower each one to provide the strongest, cleanest sound without buzzing and at a height that makes the bass comfortable to play. With your string action gauge, measure from the top of the 15th fret wire (or where it would be on a fretless bass) to the bottom of each string. Below are the tolerances in millimeters and inches as recommended by Fender. Note that you will need to know the neck radius of your bass, and that the larger ones refer to a 5- or 6-string bass.

Neck Radius	String Height – Bass Side	String Height – Treble Side
7.25"	7/64" (2.8 mm)	6/64" (2.4 mm)
9. 5" to 12"	6/64" (2.4 mm)	5/64" (2.0 mm)
15" to 17"	6/64" (2.4 mm)	5/64" (2.0 mm)

String height at the nut is equally important. As on a guitar, check by pushing each string down so it touches the top of the 3rd fret wire; it should then just barely touch the 1st fret wire. If the nut is too low, or the slots are too deep, the heavier strings, in particular, will buzz when you play notes at the 1st fret. If the nut is too low, it may need to be shimmed to raise it. In the worst case scenario, a new nut must be made. Either way, it's a job for a skilled repairman, as you could do damage removing the old nut. After making all these adjustments, intonate the bass using the same method as with a guitar.

PICKUP LINES

Bass pickup adjustments are virtually the same as on the guitar. However, where as rock, blues, and some pop guitarists generally want maximum volume from their instrument by raising their pickups as close to the strings as possible to contribute to a desired overdriven sound, jazz bass players, for example, may opt for a cleaner sound. In that case, bass pickups should be gradually raised until the desired degree of sensitivity, along with clarity, is reached when played through an amp. Be aware, however, that due to the bigger circumference of bass strings and the larger allowance needed for their wider vibrations, having bass pickups too close to the strings can make for weird, unwanted tones—particularly in the higher registers.

CHAPTER 7:

Tales from the Road– Troubleshooting and Quick Repairs

In 1998, I was in Staten Island, NY working on a B-52s show, with whom I had been touring for about six years. The gig was part of an MTV concert series where a band would play outside in a contest winner's backyard. While we were getting ready for sound check, a strong wind started to blow. The trees were swaying, and dirt and debris were blowing all around and blinding us. We started to cover up the gear, but the wind was so strong it was impossible to keep anything covered. It was happening very quickly, and I realized that this was a very serious situation. I shouted to my fellow techs, "Get the f**k off the stage now!!" There was a house about 50 yards from the stage, and we ran for our lives.

We got inside just in time to see a tornado cutting through the field and across the stage! The gear was getting blown all over and soaked by the rain. Parts of the house were even being torn off! We looked out the window helplessly, watching our gear getting trashed. The band's drummer came up to our drum tech, Eric Anderson, and said "Hey man, go get my drums." I don't have to repeat what Eric's response was. Nobody in their right mind would have gone out in that storm.

The storm passed, and we went back onstage to assess the damage. My guitar rig was trashed. We were using a Rocktron midi patching system for Keith Strickland to access

Tech Tip: Making a List and Checking It Every Day

On the afternoon before a show when I am restringing guitars, I always perform the following:

- Make sure the lock nut on each tuning machine is tight against the washer next to the headstock

- Tighten the adjusting screw on the tuning button if necessary, so it is snug, but not too tight

- Check the bridge for corrosion, excessive wear, or to see if it's collapsing

- Play the guitar through an amp or a headphone amp to make sure the pickups and controls are working

- Make sure the jack is making a good connection with the plug on the cable, applying De-Oxit if necessary

- Check the frets for excessive wear

In addition, I check the nut to confirm that none of the slots are worn too deep by pushing each string down on the 3rd fret wire to see if there is sufficient clearance above the 1st fret. If any string is touching at the 1st fret, there will be buzzing. On acoustics, I'll use an inspection mirror (like the dentist uses) to look inside the sound hole and observe the condition of the braces. I'll also tap on the top and listen for the rattle of any loose braces.

his effect pedals, and I didn't have time to fix it; I really didn't know what the problem was—other than that the rig was soaking wet. I had to take all of the pedals out of the rack and quickly make a small pedal board to get Keith through the show. He had to re-learn the system since he was used to using presets on his pedal board. It wasn't an easy show for us, but we got through it. Unfortunately, it was on live TV!

THE WIZARD BEHIND THE CURTAIN

Besides being able to maintain and repair guitars and amps, one of the most important parts of my job has been to troubleshoot problems and fix them fast! Ideally, this is done without a single note being missed or me having to be seen onstage. Things go wrong, but it's my job to do everything possible to prevent any type of technical malfunction. It's up to me to think ahead and have everything in perfect working order so the musician does not have to think about his gear.

I rely on instinct a lot. I've seen many problems in the past and have learned from past mistakes. One lesson I learned early on is there is always something new to learn and always somebody who knows more than you. Your band could be playing in front of 20 people quietly drinking wine and having dinner or before 50,000 screaming fans in a football stadium. With most of the bands, we often do live TV performances where you don't get a second chance to fix something once the cameras are rolling. Whatever you do has to work because you have no choice. In these days of YouTube, you don't want a video of a bum performance to go viral. When you're onstage and something goes wrong and everyone is looking at you, you'll quickly become a hero or look like a fool. So, you really have to act fast and be cool.

Tech Tip: Be a Troubleshooting Detective

If you're getting no sound, the first thing to do is make sure the amp is plugged in and the volume is turned up! You'd be amazed how often that is the solution. If there's still no signal from the guitar, try and recreate the problem. Shake the guitar cable or the ones connecting the effects to see if they make any static or crackling noises and are breaking the signal chain. If the cables are functioning properly, next plug the guitar directly into the amp to make sure both are working okay. If that checks out, start testing each pedal one at a time between the guitar and amp. If you find one that does not work, try a fresh battery or plug it into an adaptor. If you're dealing with one of the Bradshaw-style racks, you want to make sure every day that everything is plugged in. Sometimes you just need to do what we call a "power cycle," which is just a matter or turning everything off and on again—sort of like rebooting your computer. A cable tester and a multimeter, as previously mentioned, are essential troubleshooting tools.

Another important thing is to always wear black clothes onstage. You don't want to stand out. Nobody other than your mom is there to see you, and I always say to mine, "If you see me during the show, it means there's something wrong!" Realize also that you need to be constantly prepared to deal with less than ideal conditions. I've been through windstorms, tornadoes, heavy rain, lightning storms, extreme heat, and everything in between. Drastic weather changes can and will affect equipment, and so you need to be prepared for that. The electricity in the venue may be bad, or you might be dealing with a hung over guitar player. You never know what might come up!

Tech Tip: DIY!

I make my own guitar cables and usually each patch cable between the effects, too. If I make them, I know they're good. It's handy to make a cable "loom" and to use cable ties so that they are all wrapped neatly together in one long "snake" and cut to length, instead of having them running separately all over onstage. I also save a lot of time by labeling each one with a label maker so I immediately know where they go. You can do it by color too so that you know that red goes to red, etc.—like hooking up audio equipment or a DVD player.

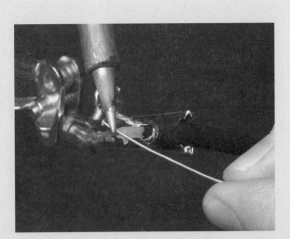

Keep the plugs on the cables clean by spraying them with Cramolin. I've learned how to solder and have a really good soldering iron as well. It takes a lot of practice to get good at it, but it's an invaluable skill to acquire. If you cannot solder, you cannot do this job.

FOLLOW THE SCOUT MOTTO

Be prepared! It is really important to think about what you will do if a piece of equipment breaks down and to have a backup plan. You must have backups for every piece of equipment or a suitable replacement. A typical situation is when a musician walks into the sound check and nothing works. We call that "gremlins." So, you need to think ahead. What if an amp breaks down, a guitar string or a strap button breaks, a pedal board loses power, or an effect stops working in the middle of a show? First of all, you need a thorough knowledge of the gear and of the signal path between the guitar and the amp—where it starts, where it ends, and everything in between. I like to draw a diagram of the setup, almost the way a plumber has a blueprint of the pipes and drains. I study it, learn it, and keep it handy.

A STRAPPING ISSUE

Early on I was doing a gig with Echo & the Bunnymen and was tuning onstage before the show with Will Seargent's beautiful 12-string Rickenbacker. It was his favorite guitar. As I was tuning it, the screw holding in the top strap button came out, and the guitar fell down with a "clunk" right in front of the audience. Fortunately, I was able to prevent it from hitting the floor because I got my foot under the headstock just in time, though it smashed my toe. Not only was it incredibly embarrassing, but I had to quickly retune the guitar and get a strap button back on before the show started.

You can use toothpicks to make a quick and long-lasting repair on a strap button where the screw has become loose in its hole. Place two or three together

Tech Tip: Button It Up

Strap locks on your guitars are essential security and should be used all the time.

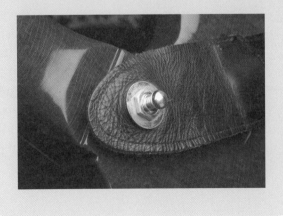

and wood glue them into the screw hole. Cut them off smoothly and evenly with the body of the guitar and let the glue dry for a little while. Put some soap on the screw as a lubricant and screw it right back in with the strap button. The ideal length of time to dry is 24 hours, but I've done this during shows, and it will hold.

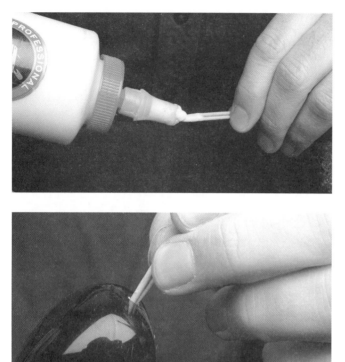

Tech Tip: Drink and Lock

The red rubber gasket on the caps of some Grolsch beer bottles can work in a pinch to keep your guitar strap on the button. Another quick, temporary fix can be made with the plastic tabs (with the price and expiration date) found on some loaves of bread to seal the plastic wrap.

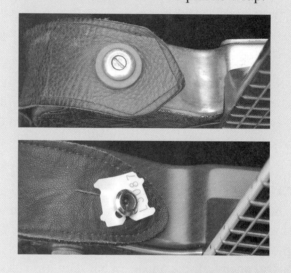

Always make sure to check that the strap button screws are tight. Strap locks are highly recommended. On vintage guitars, I use the Dunlop plastic strap locks so I don't have to replace the vintage parts.

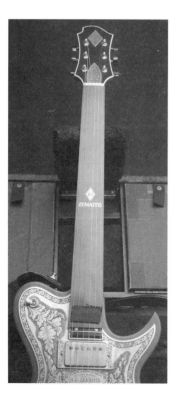

FEAR OF FLYING

When flying with guitars or when shipping them, the question arises as to whether to de-tune the strings due to the lack of air pressure. The only ones on which that is necessary are Gibson-type guitars with the headstock that slants back from the nut, because it is a weak area that's prone to cracking. So I de-tune them a whole step. This is not necessary on Fender-type guitars with the straight back headstock. Another thing I do when guitars are transported is to place sheets of cardboard between the strings and the fretboard, as guitars tend to move around in their cases. The cardboard protects the frets from having the strings rub against them in transit. It's always a good idea to have quality cases for your guitars. Guys will sometimes spend thousands of dollars on a guitar and then put it in an old, beat up case. Get a good case when you are checking your guitar with the airlines—one that is TSA approved.

CHAPTER 8:
Humidity and Your Acoustic Guitar

Humidity affects you and your acoustic guitar. However, where *you* can adapt to too much or too little by changing your environment with little or no residual effect, your prize flat top may suffer serious damage. Either too much or too little is bad. Recommended is 40 to 50 percent relative humidity as measured with a hygrometer.

Tech Tip: Ship Ahoy

Sailors, as well as meteorologists, check hygrometers to note weather changes. Hygrometers are often seen paired with thermometers, and cheap, effective ones may be purchased in hardware or household items stores. However, a digital hygrometer is more accurate and convenient.

Low humidity, as often occurs in Northern climes in the winter when the heat comes on in apartments, may crack the finish on the top, sides, back, and the neck of an acoustic guitar. While not necessarily structurally harmful, it will mar the appearance of your instrument and is virtually impossible to correct, barring refinishing. Other issues that may occur from low humidity that affect playability, including intonation and tuning problems, are fretboard shrinkage (causing sharp fret ends), loose braces, string buzzing in the higher register, reverse neck bow (easily cured by a truss rod adjustment), having the top of your guitar sink, and the bridge pulling up.

Tech Tip: Lift Off

Examine the bridge. If you can slip a paper guitar string wrapper under it, it must be removed and re-glued by a professional.

Though it's rarer than too little humidity, too much humidity is also bad, as it can result in the top of your guitar swelling and producing high action. To counter this, some guitarists install a lower saddle in the summer when in humid climates.

TAKE PRECAUTIONS

Common sense often dictates how to protect your acoustic from humidity problems:

- Never leave your guitar unattended in a car or the trunk in cold or hot weather when traveling. (Never leave your guitar unattended in the trunk or inside the car, period!)
- The best protection for your guitar is to keep it in its case when not being played.

- If you keep your acoustic guitars out in a room, use a room humidifier with a warm mist. Your sinuses will appreciate it as well.

- When bringing an acoustic guitar from a cold car or truck into a warm environment, let it sit in its case for at least one-half hour. Then open the case slowly and fan in some room air with your hand.

- Keep your fretboard oiled and clean, especially in the winter. Clean the frets with 0000 steel wool.

Tech Tip: Water Works

The Dampit and the Kyser Lifeguard humidifiers that fit inside the sound hole are a good choice for keeping your acoustic hydrated in winter and/or dry conditions. Both have a sponge inside that is to be filled with tap water. Be careful to squeeze out the excess water before installing as per instructions; the last thing you want is water dripping inside the body of your hollow wooden axe. The Dampit holds more water, but you must take care that the hose does not lie against the bottom or sides of your instrument. The Kyser holds less water but is easier and more convenient to use. On the road I use a Planet Waves Humidipak Automatic Humidity Control System, which does not need water and automatically hydrates and dehydrates the guitar.

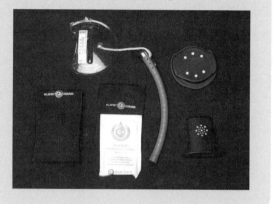

CHAPTER 9:
Amp Care and Maintenance

I was with kd Lang in Sydney, Australia, the band was about to come onstage, and I had gone through all my pre-show checks. All of the guitars, amps, pedal boards, and keyboards were working, and everything was fine. The house lights went out, the band walked onstage, and everyone started to play. Grecco Burrato, k.d.'s guitar player, started waving to me. Something was wrong, and there was no sound coming out of his amp! I immediately started sweating and ran out onstage. I checked his pedal board and saw there were no lights lit on any of the pedals, meaning there was no power going to any of his effects! I unplugged his guitar cable from the pedal board and plugged him straight into the amp. We got sound at that point, and fortunately the band didn't have to stop playing.

The culprit? He had a Voodoo Labs power supply on the pedal board (an old one), which was powering all of his pedals, and it had blown up! I immediately knew that was the problem because when I touched it, I burnt my hand—it was that hot! Next, I had to figure out how to get the pedals working. Luckily, I had individual power supply adaptors or batteries for each effect, and I was able to get them all working after one song. The show must go on, and luckily it did!

Tech Tip: You've Got the Power

When traveling abroad, we use step down transformers to convert the US 110–120 volts to the 220–240 volts in Europe and Australia. But there's another problem that you must be aware of when doing this: transformers and converters only convert the voltage—not the cycles. North American 110–120 volt electricity is generated at 60 Hz (cycles), and most international 220–240 volt electricity is generated at 50 Hz (cycles). The problem with this is that equipment can burn out after a while, depending on the quality of the insulation of the electrical wiring. It's also important to know this will greatly affect the sound of a Hammond B-3 organ—something I learned the hard way! Trec II Products makes a frequency conversion unit (SC-60D-1 for self-starting organs and SC-60D-2 for non-self-starting) that's needed to allow the organ to play precisely in tune when you don't have the 60hz. You must have this installed when using your American-made Hammond abroad. (**WARNING!** All amp repairs should be done by reputable repairmen, and the authors take no responsibility for injuries that may occur from poking around inside an amp head.)

Tech Tip: A Shocking Revelation

Whenever you perform any maintenance on your amps, be sure the power cord is unplugged from the wall. In addition, always keep one hand behind your back or in your pocket when changing tubes or performing any work on your amp. This will prevent the possibility of a dangerous shock that could occur if you have both hands on the amp, thereby completing the electrical circuit. Likewise, never work on your amp in bare feet, when standing in a puddle, or while in the bathtub!

AMP WORDS TO LIVE BY

Before you begin any maintenance or adjustment on your amp, you should have in your possession Aspen Pitman's *The Tube Amp Book* (see Chapter 10). Next, you should know that amps basically fall into two categories: tube and solid state (or transistor). The latter are harder to work with, as there are few components that can be changed by the user. About the only thing you can do yourself is to check for the ribbon connector inside and make sure it is pressed down and connected, should it bounce out during travel, resulting in poor or no sound at all. You could also look at the circuit board and see if there is anything obvious like a solder joint that has come apart. However, beyond that, a malfunctioning solid state amp will need to go to a repairman.

Inside Fender Tube Amp   Tube Layout on Fender Amp

Tube amps are far easier to maintain, as the potential problems are generally visible. These often include a burned out or broken tube, a broken fuse, or a capacitor ("filter caps") that has reached the end of its lifespan by leaking or expanding. Worn out filter caps are often noisy and can add an odd harmonic—like someone singing off-key—and their degradation can eventually lead to no sound at all. **WARNING!** Filter caps retain voltage even when the amp is turned off and unplugged from the wall. Leave their maintenance, and that of resistors, as well, to an experienced pro.

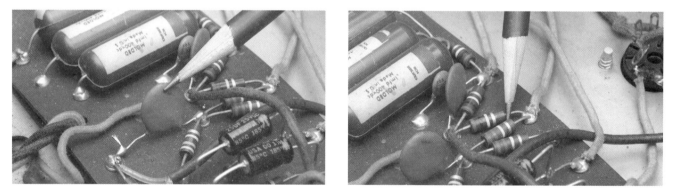

Capacitor   Resistor

Tech Tip: Tu-Be or Not Tu-Be

Solid state, or semiconductor, technology has come a long ways since the '60s—especially regarding "modeling amps," which produce a reasonable facsimile of the most popular classic tube amps for a warm, "natural" sound. Nonetheless, many guitarists believe that the most responsiveness and most desirable distortion—be it smooth or grinding—still comes from "inefficient," overheated vacuum tubes.

When I'm on the road, I always have a spare amp head or combo amp onstage right next to the one(s) being played by the artist. I've personally observed techs running right through the audience in the middle of a show to get a spare amp from the truck. You've never seen anyone sweat and run so fast! Needless to say, it's a better idea to always have a spare at the ready. It may be a luxury for some people, but out on the road or even on a gig in town, you'll be glad you were prepared.

Tech Tip: Just a Warm Up

It's always important to let the tubes and the amp warm up on "standby" at least two minutes before turning on the "play" mode and playing. When out on a gig, I'll usually turn the amps on standby during the opening act's set so that they'll be on for at least one-half hour. You can really damage a tube amp if you attempt to play them before they are warmed up—not to mention you'll significantly decrease tube life if you make a habit of it. Likewise, it's a good idea to let the amps cool down before loading out by leaving them on standby for a few minutes before shutting them off. Note: This is not necessary with transistor or solid state amps; they may be turned on and off any time.

Also, you want the amps to be at room temperature before you even turn them on standby, especially if they just came off a cold truck. Otherwise, condensation inside the amp can cause a short. Humidity is also the enemy of amps. Never store your amp in a damp garage or any other place that is not clean and dry.

CABLE NEWS

WARNING! Never, ever turn on an amp that is not plugged into a speaker. You will most likely experience major amp damage, and it will have to be serviced by a pro. Also, always use a speaker cable, known as a "balanced cable," rather than a guitar cable. If you do happen to use a guitar cable, you will likewise damage your amp. Conversely, if you use a "balanced cable" with your guitar, you'll get noise; guitar cables are "grounded" and "shielded" to protect from noise, and balanced speaker cables are not.

Tech Tip: Can You Hear Me Now?

If you aren't getting any sound out of your amp, remove anything between your guitar and amp, such as your pedals or a pedal board, and plug your guitar directly into the amp. Check to make sure the guitar cable is functioning properly, as well, and make sure the volume on the amp is up! And make sure the guitar is plugged in!

YOU(R) TUBES

It is really important to always have spare tubes. Virtually all tube amps have power amp tubes and preamp tubes, and many have a rectifier tube as well. You want to have one of every tube on hand as a backup. In addition, you also need to have matched sets of power tubes to get maximum performance from them. (This is assuming it's not a single-ended amp, which only uses one power amp tube—a rarity on the road as single-ended amps are typically lower wattage and are generally employed more often in the studio.) Whenever I'm getting ready to go on the road with an artist, I take the amps to one of my amp guys in New York City to give it a once-over, replace the tubes with a matched set of two or four (depending on the model amp), and provide me with a matched set as backups. That way I won't have to re-bias the amps if the old ones become damaged or stop functioning properly; I just switch in new tubes.

Tech Tip: We Have Your Number

Common power tubes include:

- 6L6/5881/KT66
- 6V6
- 6550
- EL34
- EL84
- 7027

Common preamp tubes include:

- 12AT7
- 12AU7
- 12AX7/7025
- 12AY7

Common rectifier tubes include:

- GZ34/5AR4
- 5U4
- 5Y3

Never mix different kinds of tubes, such as swapping out 6L6s and EL34s. The amp will not function properly and could possibly be damaged.

Preamp Tubes   *Power Tubes*

Be aware that, as of this writing, there are no vacuum tube factories in the US or UK (as there was in the past) producing high-quality RCA, Sylvania, GE, Phillips, Mullard, etc., tubes. These may still be found, however, at specialty electronics outlets and at vintage guitar shows as NOS (New Old Stock), JAN (Joint Army and Navy vintage military tubes), or even used ones that are still serviceable. Almost all modern tubes are made in Russia (Sovtek), China, and Slovakia, where they still use "primitive" technology in many applications, including military. Amp tubes are quite inconsistent these days. You want to stay away from the Chinese tubes. I get the JJ Slovakian kind and have my amp guys "burn them in" and basically check them out. However, many companies, like Groove Tubes, buy large quantities from overseas and check and match them for a premium price. Electro-Harmonix, CE Distribution, and Tube Depot are reliable sources for buying tubes.

Tech Tip: Caliente!

Before removing a tube from an amp that has been running, let it cool down. Not only can you fry your fingers, but you might also damage the tube. Number each one, so you know which socket it came from. Some older amps have a little chart pasted inside the cabinet, or you can make one yourself, labeling each tube and its location. It also doesn't hurt to put a little arrow on them with a marking pen showing the front and where they line up with the socket. Besides possibly breaking the power tubes, you might mess up the socket trying to force in the tube. With the smaller preamp tubes in particular, it's easy to bend the tiny, fragile pins.

When replacing tubes, I always change them all at the same time. However, many people don't change the preamp tubes every time the power tubes are changed, as they don't wear out nearly as fast. The one exception to this is the phase inverter tube. This will be the preamp tube that's closest to the power amp tubes (single-ended amps don't have a phase inverter tube). So some people will change the power tubes and the phase inverter tube more often than they change the rest of the preamp tubes.

Tubes are somewhat like strings: they degrade slowly over a period of time, and you sometimes don't realize how poor they sound until you put new ones in your amp. It can often sound brand new by comparison. One sure sign of old, tired tubes is a flaccid, floppy bass sound. Of course, an outright failure is hard to ignore, as you will likely have no sound at all except for perhaps an annoying electronic hum. The analogy has also been made to car tires: if one of them blows, you know eventually the others are going to fail as well. However, it's better to change all tubes before they go south! One sign that a tube is going is a high-pitched, "microphonic" squeal. The quick and easy method for checking which tube is the culprit is to tap each power tube with a Sharpie or a chopstick while the amp is on and notice the ringing tone that it emits. To further confirm which one, you can swap the tube with another in the amp and perform the same test.

Tech Tip: "Picking" Your Amp

Sometimes the retaining pins in the tube sockets get loose over time, especially in vintage amps. This may be a problem best left to a pro, but if you must, try the following: The late "Amp Doctor" Cesar Diaz suggested using a wooden toothpick to straighten out the retaining pins in the tube sockets by pushing it down in between each pin and the outer wall of the socket. Give it a try. Of course, make sure the amp is unplugged, and keep one hand behind your back. Though there is no chance of a shock when using wood or a tool with an insulated handle, it's a good habit to develop whenever working on your amp.

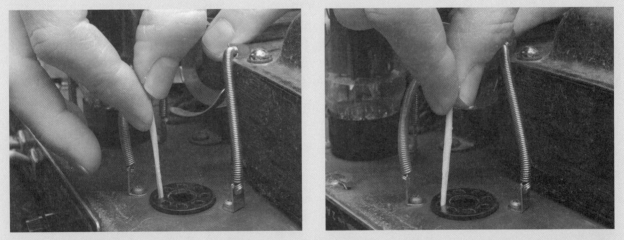

You can also help to maintain good contact in your tube sockets by using a tube socket cleaner spray sold at Radio Shack. This can be especially beneficial on an older amp. **WARNING!** Never use a lubricating spray!

Having matched sets ready to go on the road with the amps already biased is my solution for when an artist comes up to me and says, "My amp sounds muddy and dull. Where is my tone?" It's a real pain to have to bias an amp on the road, though they have biasing kits with a meter and probes. However, most amp companies do not put the bias screw in an easily accessible location.

Tech Tip: Are You Biased?

Each power tube needs a certain bias current to keep it operating at a point where the amount and type of distortion under normal conditions is well-controlled. Simply put, biasing an amp for new tubes is a way of adjusting it to match the tubes' different voltages for peak performance and longevity. If the tubes are under-biased, your amp will distort earlier. If over-biased, it will take higher amp volume to distort. Be aware, however, that either situation may lead to amp damage. Note: Preamp tubes do not require biasing and can be switched out without any adjustment needed. **WARNING!** Though relatively quick and simple to do with the proper equipment and experience, biasing should only be done by skilled technicians and is not a user-friendly maintenance.

Another way to tell bad tubes is by a "frosting" on the glass. Also if the tube is glowing bright red, as opposed to blue, this can be a sign of a dying tube. Something else I have seen sometimes is what I call a tube going "nuclear," where the protons and neutrons are going crazy in the tube. As soon as you see that, turn the amp off, because there is going to be a big pop soon.

If you do have a tube blow, you should also remove and check the fuse to make sure it has not blown as well. Sometimes you'll see black soot or carbon residue in the tube socket, which means the tube "arced" or "exploded" in the socket. You must clean off this residue before installing a new tube because you now have "conduction" building between the tube and the socket. Sometimes the socket must be replaced by a repairman, as it may just keep blowing tubes if it is damaged beyond a cleaning.

Tech Tip: Ex-fuse Me?

When tubes go, they often take a fuse with it. For every amp I have in my care, I keep the proper fuse taped to the inside of the cabinet. It's extremely important to have the proper fuse, as it can save your gig. **WARNING!** If you do not have the correct fuse, **never** go higher in amperage! If you have a serious electrical problem, it can result in the amp burning out. If you must try a different fuse than the one rated for the amp, always go lower. Sometimes you can't tell a blown fuse by looking at it, in which case you can use your multimeter to check the continuity.

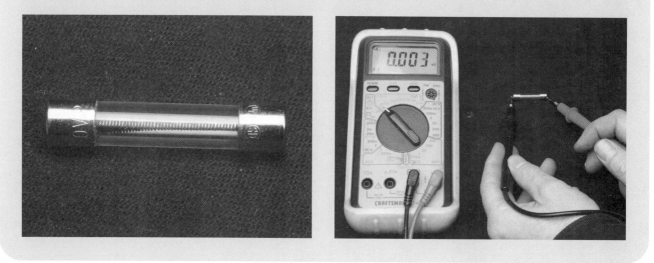

TWISTING THE NIGHT AWAY

The volume and tone knobs, or potentiometers, on an amp will give many years of service if lubricated regularly. I recommend DeoxIT, which is made by Caig. You can use it for amp and guitar "pots" if they get scratchy or do not turn as smoothly and freely as they should. Spray it inside the pot, twist the knob a few times, and it should clean it up in a second. If that doesn't work, the pot may need to be replaced.

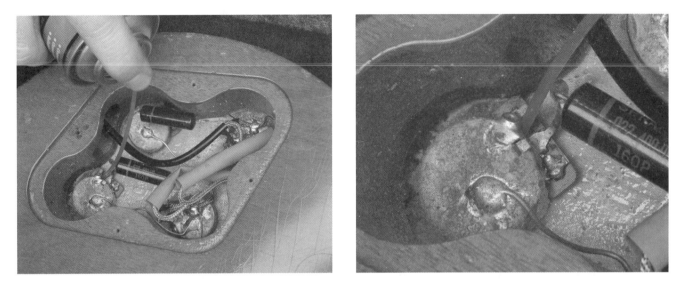

IN THE TANK

If possible, when out on the road it's recommended to carry a spare spring reverb tank—especially for your Fender amps. They really get bounced around in the truck, and if those thin, little springs get damaged, they are impossible to fix. It's very easy to swap them out, but really hard to repair them. Electro-Harmonix in Long Island City, New York, has them.

GET GROUNDED

This can be a complicated topic, as the whole grounding thing is a science, and there are guys who are really good at it. Sometimes when we're using two amps, we'll get a buzzing noise and will "ground lift" one amp. That means using one of those gray adaptors that convert a three-prong "grounded" plug on the end of the amp power cord to a two-prong, "ungrounded" plug to be plugged into the socket. That way, one amp will be grounded, and the other will not, hopefully solving the buzzing problem. Whenever I use a ground lift adaptor on an amp, I always make sure to meter the voltage between the guitar's jack or strings and the artist's microphone. You don't want to kill your guitar player! (Well, most of the time, anyway.) A simple test is to touch the guitar strings to the microphone. If it makes a pop, then you have a grounding problem. But, I would rather just meter the strings to the microphone to make sure there is no voltage going through.

Some guys like using a "variac," which brings down the voltage like a "power soak," allowing you to achieve heavy distortion at lower volume levels. Eddie Van Halen helped to popularize the technique with his sound on Van Halen's debut album and Steve Stevens used to do it—it was a big part of his sound, however, every amp person I know advises against this.

Tech Tip: Stand Your Ground

In sound recording and reproduction, "ground lift" or "earth lift" is a technique used to reduce or eliminate ground-related noise when connecting signal lines between two or more pieces of equipment. It interrupts the ground line at some point and is particularly effective at eliminating ground loops, although it may also increase or decrease noise from other sources. **WARNING!** Removal of the safety ground connection on equipment can expose users to an increased danger of electric shock and may contradict wiring regulations. The safety ground is disconnected by an adaptor (cheater plug) in a power lead in which the ground conductor is deliberately disconnected, or by cutting a ground pin in the power plug. If a fault develops in any line-operated equipment, cable shields and equipment enclosures may become energized, creating an electric shock hazard. For example, the metal shell of a stage microphone or the strings of a guitar may become energized, creating a hazard to performers. Wireless units (on microphones and guitars) eliminate this hazard. This danger is not exaggerated! Keith Relf of the Yardbirds and Leslie Harvey of Stone the Crows were both electrocuted by improperly grounded electric guitars.

SPEAK UP

Matching speaker impedance is very important, especially as regards Marshall amps when using one head with either one or two 4x12 cabinets. On the back of a Marshall amp, you'll usually see a little switch to change impedance with three choices: 4 ohms, 8 ohms, or 16 ohms. If you're only playing through one cabinet, your choice should be pretty obvious, as you will match it to the impedance appearing on the back of the cabinet. If the cabinet is missing that info, it's easy to test for it by connecting a cable to a multimeter set for ohms. When using more than one cabinet of equal ohms, you divide the impedance of one cabinet by the number being used. For example, if you have two 8 ohm cabinets, you set the impedance to 4 ohms (impedance of one cabinet, 8, divided by number being used, 2 = 4 ohms). For two 16 ohm cabinets, you set the impedance to 8 ohms, etc.

What happens when you're using two cabinets with different impedances? Let's say you have one 16 ohm and one 8 ohm cabinet. You would then set your impedance at 4 ohms. The rule of thumb is you set the impedance on the amp to **half the value of the cabinet with the lowest impedance**. You always want to make sure that your speaker cabinets have the capacity to handle the full power of your amp. In addition, all the speakers in an individual cabinet should be the same impedance, ohms, and brand.

Tech Tip: Impedance to What?

The concept of impedance matching was originally developed for electrical engineering and can be applied where a form of energy (an audio signal) is transferred between a source (amp) and a load (speakers).

IS IT JUST A PHASE?

Sometimes when we're on the road, the artist will play through two different combos, such as a Vox and a

Marshall, at the same time. In that case, you need to make sure all the speakers are "in phase" or "blowing" the same way. Speakers alternatively push out and pull in to drive the sound, and multiple speakers must be doing it in unison to produce the best sound. This is important, as sometimes guys will be standing onstage playing really loud and complaining that they cannot hear their amps. It's because the amps are "out of phase." Now, the soundman can adjust it from the sound board with a phasing switch, so that what the audience hears is in phase, but that will not help the musician onstage.

There's a simple way to make sure your speakers are all blowing the same way using a 9-volt battery and two alligator clips. Connect one end of the alligator clip to the positive battery terminal and the other

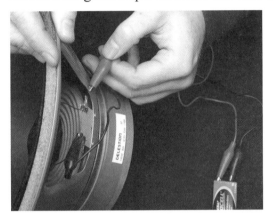

end to one of the speaker terminals (it doesn't matter which one). Now connect the other alligator clip from the negative battery terminal to the other speaker terminal. When you do this, the speaker will either move forward or backward; take notice of the result. Try the same test (make sure to use the same positive/negative alligator clip arrangement) on the other speakers. If you get a different result, then you need to change the "phase" (actually, "polarity" is the technically correct term) of that speaker. This is done by simply reversing the leads on the speaker cable so that it blows in the same direction as the others.

Tech Tip: Blow Your Horn

The battery test for speaker phasing is also a good way to test if your speaker is blown, should you be experiencing problems with it. If the speaker is frozen, the cone will not move at all. Another way is to take the speaker out of the amp and carefully push down on the cone. If it does not move, or it feels tight or gritty, that's a sign that it either needs a pro repair or has to be replaced. Of course, rips or tears in the speaker cone itself are also a bad sign, as are dents in the cap in the middle of the speaker.

OPEN- OR CLOSED-BACK SPEAKER CABINET?

An open-back cabinet will more widely disperse the sound for a bigger, more "open" sound. However, it will also usually piss off the bassist, keyboardist, and drummer onstage if they are behind the guitar amp, so you may end up putting a baffle behind the amp, anyway. Closed-back cabinets tend to have a tighter, more focused sound.

Tech Tip: Take It Off

Many musicians feel that taking the back panel off a closed back cabinet, especially on very small amps, improves the bass and treble response, as well as making the amp sound larger.

CHAPTER 10:
Resources

GUITAR REPAIR SCHOOLS
Galloup School of Guitar Building and Repair: www.galloupguitars.com
Roberto-Venn School of Luthiery: www.roberto-venn.com

BOOKS
Guitar Player Repair Guide by Dan Erlewine (Dan also has many instructional DVDs on guitar repair and maintenance available from Stew-Mac)
Complete Guitar Repair by Hideo Kamimoto
The Complete Guide to Guitar and Amp Maintenance by Ritchie Fliegler
Hal Leonard Guitar Method – Guitar Setup & Maintenance by Chad Johnson
The Tube Amp Book by Aspen Pittman
How to Service Your Own Tube Amp: A Complete Guide for the Curious Musician by Tom Mitchell
Tube Amp Talk for the Guitarist and Tech by Gerald Weber
Guitar Setup, Maintenance & Repair by John LeVan
Classic Guitar Construction by Irving Sloane (Diagrams, photographs, and step-by-step instructions)
Do-It-Yourself Projects for Guitarists by Craig Anderton
Guitar Electronics for Musicians by Donald Brosnac
The Guitar Pickups Handbook by Dave Hunter
Guitar Electronics: Understanding Wiring and Diagrams by T.A. Swike
Gruhn's Guide to Vintage Guitars by George Gruhn and Walter Carter
Guitar Identification by A.R. Duchossoir
Vintage Guitar Price Guide by Alan Greenwood

VIDEOS/DVDS
Guitar Setup & Maintenance with Denny Rauen
More Guitar Setup & Basic Modifications with Denny Rauen

TOOLS, REPAIR, AND PARTS
Stewart-MacDonald's Guitar Shop Supply
21 N. Shafer St., P.O. Box 900, Athens, OH 45701
Phone: (800) 848-2273 Fax: (740) 593-7922
www.stewmac.com

Luthiers Mercantile International, Inc.
7975 Cameron Dr. Bldg. 1600, Windsor, CA 95492
www.lmii.com

Allparts
13027 Brittmoore Park Drive, Houston, TX 77041
Phone: (713) 466-6414
www.allparts.com

WD Music Products, Inc.
4070 Mayflower Rd., Ft. Myers, FL 33916
Phone: (941) 337-7575 Fax: (941) 337-4585
www.wdmusicproducts.com

Warmoth Guitar Products
6424 112th St., E. Puyallup, WA 98373
www.warmoth.com

USA Custom Guitars
www.usacustomguitars.com

BuildYourGuitar.com
www.buildyourguitar.com

GUITAR SALES AND REPAIR SHOPS IN NYC
30th St. Guitars NYC
www.30thstreetguitars.com

David Gage String Instruments
www.davidgage.com

Manny Salvador
(repairman and luthier at David Gage String Instruments)
Phone: (646) 483-7218

GUITAR SALES AND REPAIR SHOPS IN LOS ANGELES

Truetone Music
www.truetonemusic.com

Bill Thomson
www.thomsonrentrepair.com

AMP REPAIR IN LOS ANGELES

Bob Dixon
www.amphole.com

GUITAR AND AMP COMPANIES

Martin Guitars
www.martinguitar.com

Gibson
www.gibson.com

Fender
www.fender.com

Freedom Custom Guitar Research (Japan)
www.freedomcgr.com

Ampeg
www.ampeg.com

Vox
www.voxamps.com

Marshall
www.marshallamps.com

GUITAR PICKUPS

Seymour Duncan
www.seymourduncan.com

Lindy Fralin Pickups
www.fralinpickups.com

Lollar Guitar Pickups
www.lollarguitars.com

GUITAR STRINGS AND ACCESSORIES

D'Addario
www.daddario.com

Planet Waves
www.planetwaves.com

Ernie Ball
www.ernieball.com

GHS
www.ghsstrings.com

Dean Markley
www.deanmarkley.com

Jim Dunlop
www.jimdunlop.com

Strings and Beyond
www.stringsandbeyond.com

Same Day Music
www.samedaymusic.com

MISCELLANEOUS

Crewspace
(pro road crew jobs)
www.crewspace.com

Roadie.net
www.roadie.net

Get Better at Guitar

...with these Great Guitar Instruction Books from Hal Leonard!

101 GUITAR TIPS
INCLUDES TAB

STUFF ALL THE PROS KNOW AND USE

by Adam St. James

This book contains invaluable guidance on everything from scales and music theory to truss rod adjustments, proper recording studio set-ups, and much more.

00695737 Book/Online Audio $16.99

AMAZING PHRASING
INCLUDES TAB

by Tom Kolb

This book/audio pack explores all the main components necessary for crafting well-balanced rhythmic and melodic phrases. It also explains how these phrases are put together to form cohesive solos. The companion audio contains 89 demo tracks, most with full-band backing.

00695583 Book/Online Audio $19.99

ARPEGGIOS FOR THE MODERN GUITARIST
INCLUDES TAB

by Tom Kolb

Using this no-nonsense book with online audio, guitarists will learn to apply and execute all types of arpeggio forms using a variety of techniques, including alternate picking, sweep picking, tapping, string skipping, and legato.

00695862 Book/Online Audio $19.99

BLUES YOU CAN USE

by John Ganapes

This comprehensive source for learning blues guitar is designed to develop both your lead and rhythm playing. Includes: 21 complete solos • blues chords, progressions and riffs • turnarounds • movable scales and soloing techniques • string bending • utilizing the entire fingerboard • and more.

00142420 Book/Online Media.................................$19.99

CONNECTING PENTATONIC PATTERNS
INCLUDES TAB

by Tom Kolb

If you've been finding yourself trapped in the pentatonic box, this book is for you! This hands-on book with online audio offers examples for guitar players of all levels, from beginner to advanced. Study this book faithfully, and soon you'll be soloing all over the neck with the greatest of ease.

00696445 Book/Online Audio $19.99

FRETBOARD MASTERY
INCLUDES TAB

by Troy Stetina

Untangle the mysterious regions of the guitar fretboard and unlock your potential. This book familiarizes you with all the shapes you need to know by applying them in real musical examples, thereby reinforcing and reaffirming your newfound knowledge.

00695331 Book/Online Audio $19.99

GUITAR AEROBICS
INCLUDES TAB

by Troy Nelson

Here is a daily dose of guitar "vitamins" to keep your chops fine tuned! Musical styles include rock, blues, jazz, metal, country, and funk. Techniques taught include alternate picking, arpeggios, sweep picking, string skipping, legato, string bending, and rhythm guitar.

00695946 Book/Online Audio $19.99

GUITAR CLUES
INCLUDES TAB

OPERATION PENTATONIC

by Greg Koch

Whether you're new to improvising or have been doing it for a while, this book/audio pack will provide loads of delicious licks and tricks that you can use right away, from volume swells and chicken pickin' to intervallic and chordal ideas.

00695827 Book/Online Audio $19.99

PAT METHENY – GUITAR ETUDES
INCLUDES TAB

Over the years, in many master classes and workshops around the world, Pat has demonstrated the kind of daily workout he puts himself through. This book includes a collection of 14 guitar etudes he created to help you limber up, improve picking technique and build finger independence.

00696587...$15.99

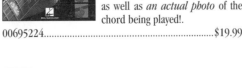

PICTURE CHORD ENCYCLOPEDIA

This comprehensive guitar chord resource for all playing styles and levels features five voicings of 44 chord qualities for all twelve keys – 2,640 chords in all! For each, there is a clearly illustrated chord frame, as well as *an actual photo* of the chord being played!.

00695224...$19.99

RHYTHM GUITAR 365
INCLUDES TAB

by Troy Nelson

This book provides 365 exercises – one for every day of the year! – to keep your rhythm chops fine tuned. Topics covered include: chord theory; the fundamentals of rhythm; fingerpicking; strum patterns; diatonic and non-diatonic progressions; triads; major and minor keys; and more.

00103627 Book/Online Audio $24.99

SCALE CHORD RELATIONSHIPS
INCLUDES TAB

by Michael Mueller & Jeff Schroedl

This book/audio pack explains how to: recognize keys • analyze chord progressions • use the modes • play over nondiatonic harmony • use harmonic and melodic minor scales • use symmetrical scales • incorporate exotic scales • and much more!

00695563 Book/Online Audio $14.99

SPEED MECHANICS FOR LEAD GUITAR
INCLUDES TAB

by Troy Stetina

Take your playing to the stratosphere with this advanced lead book which will help you develop speed and precision in today's explosive playing styles. Learn the fastest ways to achieve speed and control, secrets to make your practice time really count, and how to open your ears and make your musical ideas more solid and tangible.

00699323 Book/Online Audio $19.99

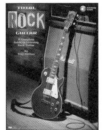

TOTAL ROCK GUITAR
INCLUDES TAB

by Troy Stetina

This comprehensive source for learning rock guitar is designed to develop both lead and rhythm playing. It covers: getting a tone that rocks • open chords, power chords and barre chords • riffs, scales and licks • string bending, strumming, and harmonics • and more.

00695246 Book/Online Audio $19.99

Guitar World Presents
STEVE VAI'S GUITAR WORKOUT
INCLUDES TAB

In this book, Steve Vai reveals his path to virtuoso enlightenment with two challenging guitar workouts – one 10-hour and one 30-hour – which include scale and chord exercises, ear training, sight-reading, music theory, and much more.

00119643...$14.99

HAL•LEONARD®

Order these and more publications from your favorite music retailer at

halleonard.com

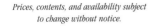